Confucian Ritual Music of Korea

Tribute to Confucius and
Royal Ancestors

Song Hye-jin   Professor Song Hye-jin is currently teaching Korean Traditional Musical History and Theory at Graduate School of Cultural Heritage Arts in Sookmyung Women's University in Seoul, Korea. She worked for Gugak FM Broadcasting where she had been deeply involved with since its inception as a chief producer from 2000 to 2004. Prof. Song received her B.A. from Seoul National University, studying Gayageum performance at the department of Korean Traditional Music. She received her M.A. and Ph.D. degrees from the Academy of Korean Studies majoring Korean Cultural Heritage arts (Traditional musical history and theory). After finishing her graduate school, she visited Durham University, England as a visiting scholar for one year.

Prof. Song had published books on Korean classical music studies including *A Study on the History of Korean Confucius Ritual Music* (2000), *Korean Musical Instruments* (2001), *Let us listen to Korean Music as this way* (2002), *History of Korean Music for Young people's* (2007) etc.

Email: hjsong@sookmyung.ac.kr

Paek In-ok   Paek In-ok is a Korean ethnomusicologist and Gayageum (long 12-string zither) player. She earned B.A. and M.A. degrees in Korean traditional music and musicology from Seoul National University and a Ph.D. in Ethnomusicology from Queen's University Belfast, Northern Ireland. She was a Leverhulme Trust Post-doctoral Research Fellow in ethnomusicology at the University of Sheffield, UK. She currently serves as a member of the Editorial Committee of the International Journal of Music Education: Practice. Her publications include co-editor and translator of *Kugak: Studies in Traditional Korean Music* by Hahn Man-young (1990), "Oral versus Written Traditions: Changing Modes in Teaching and Learning Traditional Music" (2002), "Folk Music: Vocal" (2007) and "Crossing the Border: The Gayageum Zither Tradition Amongst the Korean Minority in Northeastern China" (2008).

Confucian Ritual Music of Korea
Tribute to Confucius and Royal Ancestors
by Song Hye-jin

Published by the Korea Foundation

Translator: Paek In-ok
Copy Editor: Andrew P. Killick
Book Design & Layout: Culture Books

The Korea Foundation
Seocho P.O. Box 227
Diplomatic Center Building, 2558 Nambusunhwanno
Seoul 137-863, Korea
Tel: (82-2) 2046-8583
Fax: (82-2) 3463-6086
Email: publication@kf.or.kr

Printed in Korea

ISBN 978-89-86090-28-4 04780

Confucian Ritual Music of Korea

Tribute to Confucius and
Royal Ancestors

Song Hye-jin

Korea Foundation
한국국제교류재단

CONTENTS

III. HISTORY AND CONTEMPORARY STATUS OF KOREAN RITUAL MUSIC

INTRODUCTION

The theme of the Rite to Royal Ancestors and its accompanying music *Jongmyo jeryeak* is praying for peace. The Rite to Royal Ancestors is a composite performing art synthesizing the music, song and dance within the sacrificial rites of the Joseon Dynasty (1392-1910), which offers fervent prayers for "a great peace" through which peace reigns over the land and people enjoy the blessing of tranquility. To begin the story of the Rite to Royal Ancestors, I would like to refer to "A Bow" (*Jeol*), a poem by the poet Yi Hong-seop:

My grand uncle who spent his entire life farming / was the best person for making a polite bow. As the day for performing a sacrificial rite approaches / I often picture my grand uncle bowing / His small body curled obediently with sincerity / the appearance was such that it could not fail to impress even the spirits under the sky...

In the sacrificial rite offered to the ancestors by a farmer, "his small body curled obediently with sincerity" to the extent that "it could not fail to impress even the spirits under the sky," sincerity and devotion are essential qualities that still live on in the hearts of Koreans. This epitomizes a phrase in an old scripture stating that "the basis of ceremony is sincerity." "Devotion" (*jeongseong*) that touches the spirits under heaven was the most important element of not only the sacrificial rites performed by farmers but also those observed by the highest-ranking leaders of the country. However, there was a great difference in regard to the ceremonial procedures and contents of the sacrificial rites performed by commoners and those performed by the leaders of the country.

During my postgraduate studies (M.A. and Ph.D.), the focus of my research was the process of acceptance, acculturation and change of Chinese court sacrificial music. Since then, I have presented a number of articles covering the diverse musicological studies and methodology for musical creation that took place during the reign of King Sejong (r. 1418-1450). Furthermore, through lectures and writings on the comparative study of Chinese sacrificial music I have endeavored to inform others that the Rite to Royal Ancestors performed in Korea today is a very creative performing art form derived from the sacrificial music tradition of Northeast Asia.

The Rite to Royal Ancestors was designated as National Important Intangible Cultural Asset No.1 in 1964. To this extent, the importance of its cultural meaning and status has been emphasized in Korea. Moreover, UNESCO designated it as a World Human Oral Cultural Heritage in 2001. Nonetheless, the public has shown little interest in the Rite to Royal Ancestors and its music. In addition, the Rite to Royal Ancestors is much removed from the daily lives of modern Koreans, and the general public has difficulty understanding the music and dance as they are different from other traditional music. For this reason, I felt the need to publish an introductory book on the Rite to Royal Ancestors that is both professional and easy to comprehend. Thus, I was very excited when the Korea Foundation's proposal for a publication came through.

This book describes in detail the history of the Rite to Royal Ancestors, the general background of Confucian sacrificial music and dance, and the musical characteristics of two types of sacrificial music transmitted in Korea. The primary focus of the book is the Rite to Royal Ancestors. However, it also includes a detailed account of the Rite to Confucius in order to offer a comparison of the general traits of the tradition of Confucian ceremony in Northeast Asia that is inherent in the Rite to Royal Ancestors as well as the unique qualities that influenced its re-creation in Korea. I also gave consideration to the fact that the Rite to

Royal Ancestors is not only a ceremonial tradition that has been passed down to the present generation but also a performing art form presented in contemporary performance spaces. To help readers understand the procedures and the content of the ceremony and music, illustrations and photographic materials are included.

I sincerely hope that by focusing on the composite art form of sacrificial music this book will help readers understand the life of people in Northeast Asia who believed that a peaceful life could be attained by achieving harmony among heaven, earth and people. Finally, I would like to thank the staff of the Korea Foundation who provided me the opportunity to write the book and the editorial team.

Song Hye-jin
Summer 2008

I
INTRODUCTION TO CONFUCIAN RITUAL MUSIC

1. THE CONFUCIAN RITUAL MUSIC TRADITION IN NORTHEAST ASIA

Jeryeak is the music performed for the state Confucian ritual. Since ancient times in Northeast Asia, it has been considered important to observe filial piety to living parents and to serve them even after their death as though they were still alive through memorial rites. It was believed that performing memorial rites to the ancestors with sincere devotion would please them, thus helping their descendents to live peaceful lives generation after generation. This belief was shared by commoners and literati alike, both classes considering it a sacred duty to practice the custom of serving the ancestors in the traditional way.

In this, the king, as head of the nation, would take the lead by performing the state rituals with strict decorum. The state sacrificial rituals were basically similar to private ancestral rites in the procedure of inviting ancestral spirits, serving them reverently, and then sending them away. In other respects, however, the royal rituals were different. As the king was considered a person who received orders from heaven as well as from ancestral spirits, his rituals were based on a code of ceremony that revered heaven, the earth, and the great teachers of humankind.

Six important rituals with accompanying music and dance were performed according to fixed procedures. These were Won-gu, a rite to heaven performed by the king at the winter solstice; Sajik, a rite addressed to the guardian deities of the state such as the gods of land and grain; Jongmyo jerye, the Rite to Royal Ancestors presented to the many generations of preceding kings; Munmyo jerye, the Rite to Confucius performed at the shrine where the spirits of Confucius and other great teachers were accommodated; Seonnong, a rite for the gods of agriculture such as Sinin Sinnongssi and Hujikssi; and finally, Seonjam, a rite dedicated to Sinin Seoreungssi, the initiator of sericulture. In the

Northeast Asian cultural region, with its great emphasis on morals, ethics, and filial piety, such state rituals were transmitted as the most fundamental ceremonies for the running of the country. In Korea, the rites accompanied with music were performed from the 12th century on.

In Confucian society, performing rituals accompanied by music and dance had a particular meaning: it was not simply a matter of practicing filial piety and ethics, but also of symbolizing an era that could boast a peaceful reign and a flourishing culture. By examining the rituals of the time, it was possible to discern whether the nation was distinguished in etiquette and musical civilization or, on the contrary, in a state of corruption with degraded ceremonies and music. National leaders, therefore, always showed a particular concern for maintaining the form and content of state rituals in good order. When the state rituals were found imperfect, they would appoint experts and allocate a generous budget to improve them.

2. JERYEAK AS A FUSION OF INSTRUMENTS, SONG, AND DANCE

1) MUSICAL INSTRUMENTS (*ak*)

The instrumental music, song, and dance performed in rituals differed from those practiced privately among the people. A special arrangement of instruments had to be used. First of all, one of the principles when performing ritual music was to use instruments made from all the "eight materials" of East Asian cosmology: metal, stone, silk, bamboo, gourd, earth, leather, and wood. As these eight materials were sound-producing substances that existed in nature, it was believed that if sound were created from instruments made of each material, the music would be in har-

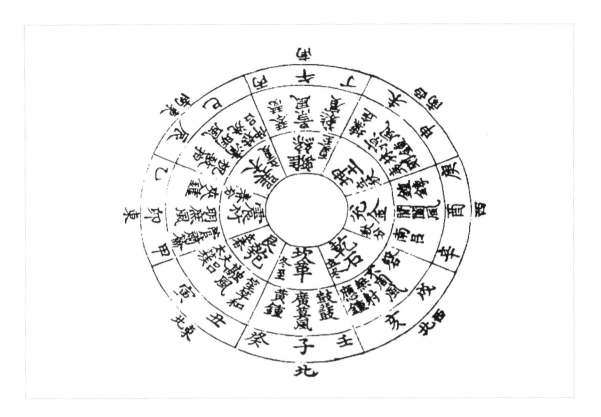

Figure 1

An illustration of pareum
(the "eight sounding materials") in the Korean musical treatise *Akhak gwe-
beom* (*Guide to the Study of
Music*, 1493).

mony just as nature was in harmony with itself; and if the instruments were played for a sacrificial rite, it would bring harmony between the gods and people like the harmony of music. In the classic texts on music, there is a saying, "*pareum geukhae sinin ihwa*." This means that only when musical instruments made of the eight materials are matched extremely well will the gods and people be in harmony.

The number and kind of musical instruments for an ensemble also depended on the recipient of the sacrificial rite and the status of the person in charge of it: the higher the social standing and rank, the greater the number and variety of instruments employed. Another noteworthy aspect of instrumental performance in ritual music is the positioning of the instruments. Sacrificial rituals require two ensembles: one positioned on higher ground near to the ancestral shrine, and the other farther away from the ancestral shrine toward the end of the courtyard. These

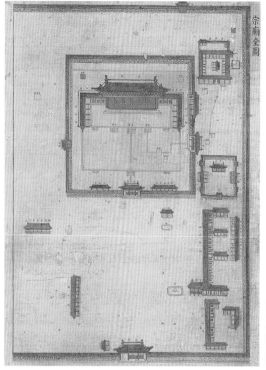

宗廟全圖

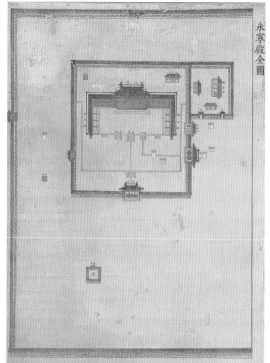

永寧殿全圖

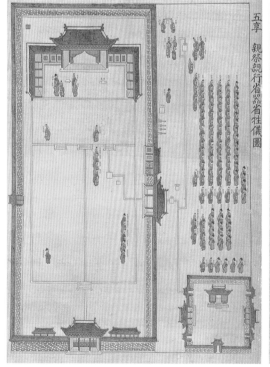

五享親祭視行省器省牲儀圖

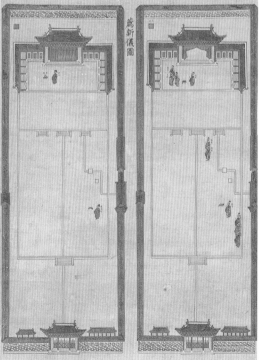

薦新儀圖

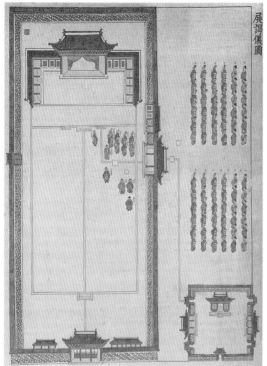

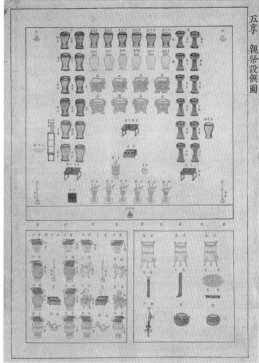

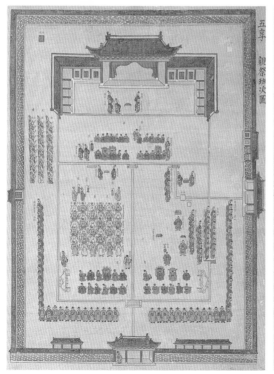

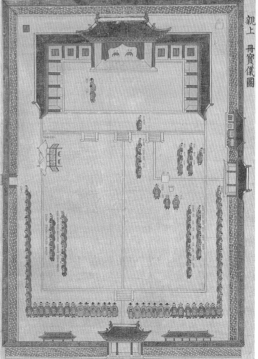

I. Introduction to Confucian ritual music • 17

Figure 2

The arrangement of the courtyard ensemble (*heon-ga*) presented in the Joseon Dynasty text *Jongmyo jerye dobyeong*.

are called *deungga* (terrace ensemble) and *heonga* (courtyard ensemble), respectively.

The terrace ensemble and courtyard ensemble symbolize *yang* (the positive cosmic force) and *yin* (the negative cosmic force), respectively, and they play alternately according to a fixed ceremonial order. The musical pieces are selected to preserve a balance between the terrace and courtyard ensembles and hence between yin and yang. For example, the courtyard ensemble, which represents yin, might choose pieces belonging to the terrace ensemble, while the terrace ensemble representing yang would select pieces with a yin character, thus promoting the balance between yin and yang. This is called the principle of yin-yang synthesis.

The consideration of social standing and rank in the orchestral formation reflects the Confucian value system with its emphasis on hierarchical order. Performance by the two alternating musical ensembles, on the other hand, indicates that the sacrificial ritual is intended to promote harmony between yin and yang and between the gods and people.

2) Song (*ga*)

Song is central to a sacrificial ritual. It is song that explicitly expresses the devotion and praise which is presented to the gods. One of the song texts from the old sacrificial rites reads:

> The great god of heaven does not give commands lightly. Where there is virtue, it flourishes. Several of our highly revered kings received wonderful commands, and by bringing the divine plans and glorious achievements to magnificent fruition, they continued to flourish. By responding to fortune, they brought the blessing of peace, nurtured the whole nation with deep love, and opened up a

Figure 3
Singers singing a hymn
(*akjang*) at the Royal
Ancestral Shrine.

bright future for succeeding generations. May this continue for ever, over a thousand million generations. How can we extol such magnificent deeds? Naturally we sing and offer our praises.

This could be regarded as the *raison d'être* of songs in sacrificial rites.

Songs sung in the sacrificial rites are called *akjang* (hymns). Their texts are Sino-Korean poems appropriate to the ritual procedure. In the procedures for welcoming a god, offering presents and food, taking up the ceremonial utensils, and sending off the god, songs of prayer are sung with words such as "We offer these sacrificial rites courteously and with sincere devotion. Please accept our sacrificial rites, and grant the descendants who are offering the ceremony your peace and blessing." In the Choheon, Aheon, and Jongheon procedures (the first, second, and third offerings of wine), a glass of wine is presented three times to the subject of the rite and the songs are sung with words to the effect of "We fully appreciate how great you are, thus cherishing the memory of your noteworthy deeds one by one. Please listen to our praise." In the Rite to Royal Ancestors, the achievements of past kings are described in detail, separated into civil and military achievements.

3) Dance (*mu*)

Sacrificial rites also involve distinctive dances. In the sacrificial dance, the number of dancers and the kind of symbolic objects employed are considered more important than the beauty of the dancers' movements. The sacrificial dance is called Ilmu, literally meaning "line dance." The dancers stand in evenly spaced lines while making the movements demanded by the rite. The number of lines varies depending on the subject of the rite: 64 dancers in 8 lines for a king, 36 or 48 dancers in 6 lines for a noble lord, 16 dancers in 4 lines for a female ancestor, and 4 dancers in 2 lines for a scholar. As with the number and variety of musical instruments, the ritual expresses the hierarchical order of status by differentiating the number of dancers for a specific ritual depending on to whom the rite is being offered.

The sacrificial dance is very simple. This is because the bodily movements of the dancers are not aimed at beauty so much as they express a courteous manner exercised with decorum when serving the ancestors with a devoted mind and well-ordered movements. A classic text on Oriental music, *Akki*(*Yüeh chi*, Music section of the *Li chi* (Book of Rites), states:

Once the government of a nation is stabilized and the people's lives become peaceful, the procession and movement of sacrificial dance become orderly and even. During turbulent times, all moderation is

lost, and inevitably the dance becomes disturbed. Thus, it is possible to grasp the state of a nation through its sacrificial dance.

Figure 4
A *parilmu* dance (eight-line dance) in the contemporary Rite to Royal Ancestors.

This shows what was considered important in sacrificial dance. Accordingly, although it is a group dance, the sacrificial dance with 64 dancers shows a unique approach to dance quite different from the ideal of perfect order in mass games.

4) INSTRUMENTS, SONG, AND DANCE UNITED

Confucian state sacrificial rites can omit none of the three aforementioned components: musical instruments, song, and dance. Only when all three are joined together can one speak of *ak* (musical instruments) in a broader sense. According to *Akki*:

Basically, *ak-eum* (musical sound) originates from the human mind's response to existence. The human mind is empty and has no form, but in function it is clear and bright, reflecting objects like a mirror. When the human mind responds to something, sentiment stirs in the heart, and *sori* (sound) results in the form of speech. When these sounds and their meanings are combined, they produce changes in the degree of clarity as well as the pitch. The method of changing the sound to perform a poem as a song is called *eum* (tone), whereas to speak of establishing a *bang* (way, method) refers to the formation of tunes. Arranging these sounds and performing them with dance involving objects such as a shield and axe, or feather and fur, is called "*ak*" (music). The shield and axe are used for military dance, the feather and fur for civil dance.

This quotation contains some difficult expressions, but if read carefully, one can see that it explains the stages through which "sound" becomes "tone" and then "music." To express it more simply: By nature, the human mind is empty but not in darkness. When a sound enters the human mind, feeling is created and moves a person's heart. When this feeling is expressed in words, it becomes sound. When several sounds are combined based on the meaning of the words, it brings about a change in clarity and pitch. When the change is organized in the manner of singing poetry, it is described as tone. When these tones are performed on instruments along with dance, it produces music. The process consists of three stages: one of simple sound, one of establishing a tonal system, and the final stage of music in which poetry is sung and instruments are played accompanying dance.

It is noteworthy to see the expressions "shield and axe" and "feather and fur" used in connection with dance. These are still used in the sacrifical rites as the symbolic objects held by the dancers in military and civil dances, respectively. The fact that they are mentioned in this classic text indicates that the sacrificial music tradition has been transmitted for a long time without much change, and that the tradition of sacrificial music that survives today represents the music that was established in ancient Northeast Asia.

5) Harmony: The ultimate aim of ritual music

As described earlier, sacrificial music is a unique cultural heritage that reflects the old tradition and mode of thinking in Northeast Asia. We should now consider exactly when and why the musical system for the major state sacrificial rites came to exist.

This is closely related to the long-standing tradition in Northeast Asia whereby the order of the universe and social relationships are represented in terms of *ye* (ceremonies) and *ak* (music). Since the Zhou Dynasty of China (1122–256 BCE), people in Northeast Asia believed that *aak* (court ritual music), modeled after the phenomena of the universe and nature by a holy person, can function to cultivate people's character, to bring heaven and earth into harmony, to unite gods and humans, and to balance yin and yang. It was in this belief that rituals and music became systematized.

Figure 5
Contemporary performance of the Rite to Royal Ancestors presented by the National Center for Korean Traditional Performing Arts (Gungnip gugagwon).

The Chinese classic stated that "Music is for uniting, ceremonies for dividing" and that "Music expresses the harmony in nature, ceremonies the order in nature." That is, ceremonies are the order, and music the harmony; ceremonies classify whereas music unites; ceremonies represent the order that divides men and women, old and young, upper and lower classes, the exalted and the lowly. Music harmonizes them into one. Such statements are very relevant to the tradition of sacrificial music. It was believed that in sacrificial rites, music shared between a king and his subjects, old and young, upper and lower classes, father and son, elder brother and younger brother, would bring unity, making the people gentle, obedient, and friendly.

As music exists as a result of the human mind's response to existence, much importance was attached to the idea that etiquette and politics were connected. Confucius's response to a question about politics put forth by his disciple Zizhang can be understood in the same context:

If a man of virtue were conversant with sacrificial music, he would take it as an example and apply the principles of ritual music to politics. That is, politics is an application of the doctrines manifested in the ceremonies and their music.

This Confucian philosophy of ceremonies and music holds an important place in Northeast Asian culture as a vehicle for correcting the social order through ceremonies that exemplify a sound social ethos for human behavior, and for guiding human societies in harmony through music that promotes peaceful human sentiments. If there were ceremonies but no music, people and society would lose their harmony and become fragmented; if there were music but no ceremonies, there would be disorder. Thus, state leaders considered it most important to keep the ceremonies and music in balance.

Akki also mentions the following:

As tone is created from the human heart, music informs ethics. Therefore, someone who knows sound but does not understand tone is a beast, and someone who knows tone but does not understand music is a commoner. Only a man of virtue can properly understand music. Thus, one acquires the correct way of governing by examining sound to understand tone, by examining tone to understand music, and finally, by examining music to understand politics. Because of this, it is not possible to discuss tone with a person who does not understand sound, or to discuss music with someone who does not understand tone. By knowing music one comes closer to understanding the ceremonies. Those who have mastered the ceremonies and music are considered men of virtue.

That is to say, since music is something that only a person of virtue can understand, it is considered an important measure of one's aptitude for governing the country. Furthermore, music was classified into *chise jieum* (music of peaceful times), *nanse jieum* (music of turbulent times) and *mangguk jieum* (music of national decay). The nature and causes of each were described in detail, thus emphasizing the importance of honoring the ceremonies and music as the basis of governing the nation. Namely, the music of peaceful times is relaxed and joyful because the political conditions are harmonious; the music of turbulent times is full of resentment and rage because of political chaos; and the music of national decay is sorrowful and full of worries because of the people's suffering. Thus, it became a primary responsibility of the ruler of a country to lead people always to be responsive to elegant and righteous music.

3. RITUAL PROCEDURES AND MUSIC

As jeryeak is the music that accompanies the ritual procedures, it has an inseparable relationship with the ritual. Therefore, to understand jeryeak is to understand the ritual procedures themselves. The core procedures of a sacrificial rite are welcoming a god, entertaining the god with food and wine, and, finally, sending the god away. These procedures are called Yeongsin, Osin and Songsin. However, these are not the only procedures. There is also a sacred preparation process that takes place prior to the performance of the sacrificial rites whereby all the participants perform a ritual cleansing so as to ready their mind and body for performing a solemn ritual.

1) PREPARATION OF SACRIFICIAL RITES

First of all, we will take an example from the Joseon period (1392-1910). A steward called *jipsagwan* would perform a ritual cleansing seven days prior to the holding of the rite. After the other participants had taken a bath and put on new clothes three days before the ritual, the steward would enter the shrine and do everything necessary for preparing the ritual. During the purification period, the steward was allowed to carry on his daily business, but was prohibited from drinking alcohol excessively or eating scallions, leeks, garlic, or shallots. The participants also had to observe a detailed list of prohibitions on activities such as condoling with mourners, visiting the sick, listening to music, signing criminal death documents, or being involved in any dirty or harmful affairs. Furthermore, during the period when the sacrificial rituals were being performed, they stayed at the Royal Ancestral Shrine (Jongmyo) and devoted themselves exclusively to matters concerning the rituals. As explained in the classic text *Yejeon* (Code of Courtesy), the reason for all this was to ensure that the body and mind were in a state of reverence during the ritual.

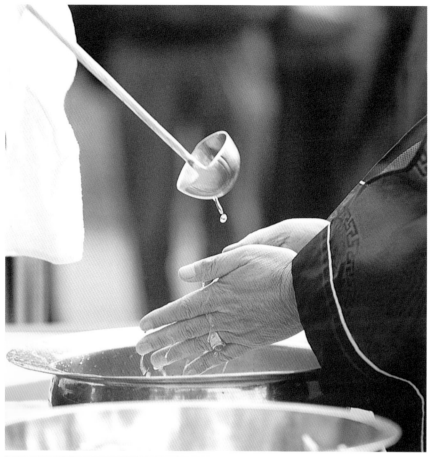

Figure 6
An officiant washing his hands (*gwanse*) at the place of ablution for the ritual

Figure 7
Officiants entering the Royal Audience Chamber for the ritual.

How have such preparation procedures changed in modern times? Currently, the Rite to Royal Ancestors is overseen the Jeonju Lee Royal Family Members Foundation (Jeonju Lee Clan Daedong Jongyagwon), which begins the preparation for the ritual by appointing a priest about two months in advance, and attends the rite in a reverent spirit after taking a bath the day before. It is noteworthy that the purification and ritual procedures have been much simplified compared to those of the Joseon period.

The Rite to Royal Ancestors proceeds according to the order specified in the *holgi* (order of service). Like a modern printed program, the holgi indicates one by one the particular points when music should begin and end, following instructions from the person conducting the ritual according to the established ceremonial procedures.

Next, we should look more closely at the actual performance of jeryeak. Once the entire preparation for the ritual was complete, the *heon-gwan*, or priest, would burn incense in the burner three times, pour wine on the ground three times, and then make the offerings (*jesu*) through the Yeongsin, Jeonpye, and Jinchan procedures.

2) *Yeongsin, Jeonpye,* AND *Jinchan*

For the Yeongsin procedure that welcomes the gods, the music is repeated nine times according to the principle of "*yeongsin gusong*" (welcoming the gods with nine completions). The reason for playing the same music nine times is not to enhance the musical effect but to show wholehearted devotion in serving the gods. Jeonpye is the procedure of offering gifts (*pyebaek*). The word "pyebaek" is still used today in reference to wedding gifts, but the pyebaek procedure for sacrificial rituals is rather different. Pyebaek means "offering gifts out of courtesy," and in wedding ceremonies it refers to the jujube or dried slices of meat sea-

soned with spices that are offered to the mother-in-law by the bride after making the ceremonial bow when they meet for the first time. It can also refer to the silks that the bridegroom presents to the bride's household before the wedding. In the Jeonpye procedure, on the other hand, pyebaek refers to a small piece of white ramie cloth that is offered to the gods on a ceremonial utensil while music is played. During the Jinchan procedure, an officiant called "*cheonjogwan*" presents food offerings on a ceremonial utensil which he places on the ceremonial table. Nowadays, the ceremonial food would be placed in advance on the ceremonial table and covered neatly. The food is offered by opening the ceremonial utensils as the Jinchan ceremony proceeds.

Figure 8
Tables set for the rite to Royal Ancestors.

Figure 9
An officiant carries the holgi that records the order of service for the Rite to Royal Ancestors.

Figure 10
The reading of the holgi during the Rite to Royal Ancestors.

3) *Choheon, Aheon,* AND *Jongheon*

These are the procedures in which a glass of wine is offered three times while singing praise songs to the subject of the ceremony. Among the three offerings, the Choheon, the first offering of wine, is the most important because this contains the procedure whereby the king or his representative offers wine to an ancestral tablet while reading a written prayer cherishing the memory of the deceased to the accompaniment of music. During the Joseon Dynasty, it used to take a long time for a single Choheon priest to offer the wine glasses and memorial prayers individually to all the ancestral tablets that are kept at the Royal Ancestral Shrine, and to enable the musical accompaniment to continue without pause, the same piece of music was played repeatedly. However, today's ritual has been condensed in that an officiant stands by at each altar and when the wine glass is offered and the written memorial prayer recited at the first altar, all the other priests carry out the first offering procedure simultaneously. The second and the third wine offerings are presented without reading the memorial prayer.

4) *Eumbok, Cheolbyeondu,* AND *Songsin*

Once the procedure of offering wine three times (collectively known as Heonjak) is completed, the Eumbok ceremony is performed. In this procedure, the steward stands at the eumbok tablet to check the wine glasses and ceremonial utensils offered to the ancestral tablets. This signifies receiving ancestral blessings through the act of eating and drinking the sacrificial food and wine. Music is not performed for this procedure. The following procedure, Cheolbyeondu, is when the offerings on the sacrificial table are taken off. Actually, they are not removed, but their positions are altered slightly. This procedure is accompanied by the playing of the deungga (terrace ensemble) without dance.

Next, the steward and all the other participants bow together four times, and then the procedure for sending off the god follows with musical accompaniment. After that, the sacrificial procedure comes to an end when the *choheon-gwan* (the steward serving the first wine offering) proceeds to the *mangnyo* tablet and burns the written prayers and sacrificial goods offered to the god. Then, all the participants leave through a designated door.

Thus, we have covered the ceremonial procedures of the Rite to Royal Ancestors from the Yongsin- Jeonpye-Jinchan sequence to the Heonjak

Figure 11
The choheon-gwan (the steward serving the first wine offering, in this case the King) presenting a ceremonial bow.

Figure 12
The choheon-gwan offering a cup of wine to the spirits.

Figure 13
A scene from the eumbok ceremony (partaking of sacrificial food and drink).

Figure 14
Burning written prayers in the concluding mangnyo ceremony.

(comprising Choheon, Aheon, and Jongheon) and the Eumbok, Cheolbyeondu, Songsin, and Mangnyo. Even after repeated explanations, it can seem very complicated. However, considering that sacrificial rites are founded on the etiquette of serving deceased ancestors as though they were still alive, we can get a general understanding of the procedures of sacrificial rites if we think of them as inviting ancestors to our home, serving them good food and wine, and then seeing them off.

RITUAL MUSIC THAT REFLECTS THE ORDER OF THE UNIVERSE

The order of the universe is reflected in jeryeak. The position of the ensembles and the performance of music and dance symbolize heaven, earth and humanity. The deungga ensemble playing on the raised terrace symbolizes heaven; the heon-ga ensemble playing in the courtyard symbolizes the earth; and the ceremonial dancers positioned to the left of the courtyard symbolize the people. The civil and military dances performed at the Rite to Royal Ancestors also reflect the order of the universe. The civil dance symbolizing *mundeok* (virtue in civil affairs) begins by lifting the left hand and foot and turning to the left. This is said to imitate the leftward movement of the Big Dipper constellation. In the military dance, which symbolizes military achievements, the dancers lift their right hands and feet and turn to the right. This imitates the sun's motion toward the right.

Likewise, the principles of the universe are also applied to ceremonial utensils and foods. For example, ceremonial utensils include *byeon*, made of finely split bamboo, and *du*, made of smoothly finished wood. The bamboo utensils symbolize yang, the wooden utensils yin. Dried foods are served in yang utensils and arranged at the east side of the altar-table, whereas watery foods are served in yin utensils and arranged at the west side of the altar-table. The food consists of 12 different kinds for each set, symbolizing the 12 months of the year. Furthermore, the ceremonial utensils are made in various shapes such as round, square, and several animal shapes. Each of these incorporates specific symbols.

Figure 15

A spear and sword
These tools are for the military dancing of a royal ancestral rite. The first two rows of dancers hold a spear and a sword in both hands, and dance during the first and last offering rites.

Yak
During the civil dancing of a royal ancestral rite, dancers hold this tool in the left hand, It is an end-blown flute.

Jeok
During the civil dancing of a royal ancestral rite, dancers hold this tool in the right hand. It is a decoration comprising a wooden dragor head from which hangs a long pendant of four phoasant feather tassels.

SUPPLEMENTARY INFORMATION

CEREMONIAL COSTUMES

The chief officiants wear royal attire with crowns and hold jade implements called *gyu*. The other officiants, called *chambanwon*, wear various ceremonial costumes determined by their rank. According to *Gyeongguk taejeon* (*National Code 1470*), the ceremonial costumes of all the government officials are divided into six kinds according to rank. Although the clothing may be the same, the coronets or personal ornaments are different. From the collapse of the Joseon Dynasty in 1910 until the beginning of the 1970s, the ceremonial costumes for the Rite to Royal Ancestors fell into decay through neglect, but greatly improved garments were worn at the Rite to Royal Ancestors held in 1976. On that occasion, Yi Gu(1931-2005), the son of Yi Un (Yeongchinwang 1897-1970), the last crown prince of Korea (the son of Gojong), took charge as the priest for Choheon. As a descendent of the last king, he wore the costume for major state ceremonies: a 12-piece royal costume and a royal

crown decorated with 12 strings of gems. He held the gyu and conducted the sacrificial rite, and the other officials and participants also wore new ceremonial costumes. In fact, the costumes had been restored according to the old system for the Rite to Royal Ancestors conducted by the king.

There are also prescribed rules for the costumes of the musicians and dancers performing jeryeak. A *jipsa* (steward) wears the same ceremonial costume as the *jegwan* (priests) because, although he is a musician, he is considered equal in status to the priests since his role is to lead the ceremonial procedures. The costume for the *jipbak* (the director of an ensemble who plays the wooden clapper) is different from that of the other musicians. He wears a hat called *bokdu*, a green robe (*cheongsam*), and a waistband made of horn. The costumes of the musicians and dancers differ between the Rite to Royal Ancestors and the Rite to Confucius. For the Rite to Royal Ancestors, all the performers wear red overcoats (*hongjuri*) and indigo waistbands. On their heads, the musicians wear *gaejeokgwan* (a hat with the top open) and the dancers wear bokdu. For the civil dance, the dancers hold an end-blown flute

Figure 16
Costume of the musical stewards (*jipsa*), conductor (*jipbak*) and musician (*aksa*) in the Rite to Royal Ancestors.

Figure 17
Costume of the civil dancers (*munmu*) in the Rite to Royal Ancestors (Joseon Dynasty).

Figure 18
Costume of the military dancers (*mumu*) in the Rite to Royal Ancestors (Joseon Dynasty).

(*yak*) in their left hand and a pheasant feather (*jeok*) in their right. For the military dance, they make a fist with their left hand and hold either a sword (*wooden geom*) or a spear (*wooden chang*) in their right hand; the front four rows of dancers hold swords and the back four rows hold spears.

For the civil dance in the Rite to Confucius, the dancers also hold a flute and pheasant feather but wear different hats called *jinhyeon-gwan*. For the military dance, they wear hats called *pibyeon-gwan* and hold a shield (*gan*) in their left hand and an axe (*cheok*) in their right.

SUPPLEMENTARY INFORMATION

WHO PERFORMS JERYEAK?

During the Joseon Dynasty, male musicians, affiliated with a national music institute called Jangagwon (Board of Music), performed the sacrificial music, while soldiers and men attached to the court who had received the proper training performed the dance. The musicians affiliated with the national music institute were classified by their status and responsibilities into *akgong*, *aksaeng* and *aksa*. The aksa was the overall director of jeryeak and was responsible for synchronizing the music and dance with the ritual by signaling with a candle (*jochok*) and flag (*hwi*). Akgong and aksaeng were responsible for instrumental performance and singing. The aksaeng performed court ritual music, such as the Rite to Confucius, while the akgong performed non-ritual music, which was divided into *hyangak* (music of Korean origin) and *dangak* (music of Chinese origin). The akgong were better paid and higher in status than the aksaeng.

Figure 19
Everlasting Sound: A Performance of the Rite to Royal Ancestors, the first performance of the reconstructed ritual music and dance of the Rite to Royal Ancestors, presented by the National Center for Korean Traditional Performing Arts in 1999.

However, during the Joseon period, the profession of musician affiliated to the Jangagwon, including aksaeng and akgong, was transmitted by heredity, and their social status was not high. With the social and political reforms of 1894 (known as the Gabo reforms), which aimed to establish a more modern social system, the hereditary system was abolished. The Jangagwon was reduced in scope and reorganized, and in the early 20th century it was re-fashioned as the Yi Wang-jik Aak-bu (The Conservatory of the Yi Royal Family). After the establishment of the Yi Wang-jik Aak-bu Yangseongso (a training institute within the Department) in 1919, members of the public who wished to become professional musicians could be selected for training and thus inherit the tradition of the Rite to Royal Ancestors from the Joseon Dynasty.

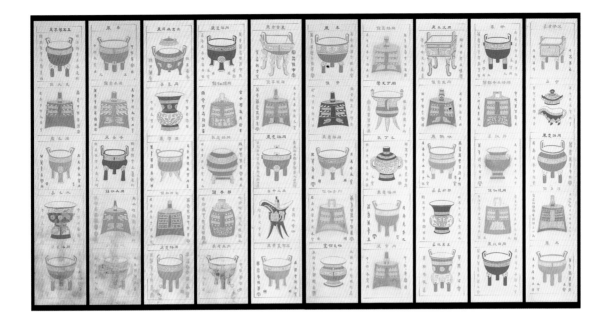

Figure 20
A 10-panel screen with paintings showing implements used in sacriticial rites in ancient China. For ancient Korean royalty and the noble class, such paintings symbolized showing obedience to the gods.

The musical tradition of the Yi Wang-jik Aak-bu was maintained throughout the Japanese colonial period (1910-1945). After the liberation of Korea from Japanese colonial rule in 1945, it became the Guhwanggung Aak-bu (Court Ritual Music Department of the Old Imperial Palace) and then the Gungnip Gugagwon (originally known in English as the National Classical Music Institute, now the National Center for Korean Traditional Performing Arts; hereafter NCKTPA), established in April 1951. In 1964, the performance of the Rite to Royal Ancestors by the musicians of the NCKTPA was designated as National Important Intangible Cultural Property No. 1. Since then, its channels of transmission have become more diverse due to the training offered at institutions such as Gugaksa Yangseongso (Traditional Music Training School), Gungnip Gugak Godeung Hakkyo (National Traditional Music High School), Gugak Junghakkyo (Traditional Music Middle School), and the Korean music departments at several universities which provide

Figure 21
Ceremonial utensils used today in the Rite to Royal Ancestors.

training for professional musicians playing traditional music. The Rite to Royal Ancestors is largely performed by the musicians at the NCKTPA and by the preservation society consisting of the appointed holders of the Intangible Cultural Property and their designated successors and students. The ritual dance is mainly performed by students at the National Traditional Music High School.

CEREMONIAL FOOD

The ceremonial food largely consists of rice, rice cakes, soup, fruits, dried slices of meat seasoned with spices, salt, pickled seafood, and rice wine, but the ceremonial utensils vary greatly in type and arrangement. According to *Jongmyo uigwe* (Record of the Rite to Royal Ancestors 1697) compiled during the reign of King Yeongjo (r. 1724-1776), the articles needed for the sacrificial rite included four kinds of cooked grains, five kinds of rice cakes, five kinds of fruit, two kinds of dried seasoned meat, four kinds of pickled seafood, seven kinds of meat dishes, four kinds of pickled vegetables, three kinds of unseasoned soup, three kinds of seasoned soup, and the usual sauces and wines. Compared to the past, the ceremonial food at present time, although modelled on past examples, has become much simplified.

In the early Joseon Dynasty, the ceremonial utensils of the Rite to Royal Ancestors were standardized in the course of revising *Yejeon* (Code of Courtesy) for national ceremonies in the light of research into Chinese classics such as *Chou li* (Book of Rites of the chou Dynasty). According to *Gukjo oryeui* (The Five National Rites 1474), the ceremonial utensils comprised 63 kinds in total, differentiated by material and shape. These included *byeon*, made of bamboo and used for dried foods; *du*, made of carved wood and used for watery foods; *jo*, used in three kinds of sacrifice; *bo* and *gwae*, containing grains; *hyeong*, containing soup; and wine glasses with distinctive shapes. The utensils for wine used in the Rite to Royal Ancestors were broadly classified into three kinds called *jun*, *i*, and *roe*. They had individual names and symbolism depending on their shape (such as cow or elephant) and their decorative designs of chicken, bird, mountain and cloud, or grains, and they also had different usages according to the seasons. The utensils for wine are particularly interesting for their symbolic meanings such as virtue, courtesy, righteousness, faith, yin and yang, and compass directions. The *sannoe*, engraved with mountain and cloud patterns, expressed the wish that, as the clouds spread rainfall far and wide, the grace of the king may extend to his people everywhere.

II
TWO KINDS OF CONFUCIAN RITUAL
MUSIC IN KOREA

1. CHINESE-STYLE COURT RITUAL MUSIC: *MUNMYO JERYEAK*

1) The Rite to Confucius and Its Music

The Rite to Confucius is a sacrificial rite for Confucius and other Confucian sages. It is performed at the Daeseongjeon shrine (Treasure No. 141), located at Seonggyun-gwan University campus in Myeongnyun-dong, Jongno-gu, Seoul. Daeseongjeon houses the memorial tablets of four great religious teachers—Confucius, Anzi, Xunzi, and Mengzi—as well as ten philosophers. At each side of the Daeseongjeon are annex buildings in which Chinese and Korean scholars are enshrined. The Rite to Confucius is performed twice a year at the equinoxes in the second and eighth lunar months along with the sacrificial rites at traditional schools all over the country, but only the ritual performed at Daeseongjeon is accompanied by music and dance.

The Rite to Confucius is also known as Seokjeondaeje. "Seokjeon" is an old name derived from the phrase "arrange (*seok*) vegetables and offer (*jeon*) gifts." Originally, in addition to the Rite to Confucius, it referred to other sacrificial rites managed by the state, such as rites to *sancheon* (mountains and streams). With the disappearance of the other sacrificial rites, however, the name Seokjeon came to refer to the Rite to Confucius exclusively.

The Rite to Confucius is a very educational ceremony in which rapport is built up between the ancient sages who inspired humankind and the younger generations who have followed in the path of learning. This rite originated from China and is performed there today, although it was greatly changed and then discontinued before being revived in the mid-20th century. In Korea, on the other hand, the tradition of ancestral sacrificial rites accompanied by music has continued without interruption

since the 12th century, and its historical significance is widely recognized. Its cultural significance can also be seen in the fact that the Rite to Confucius was the source from which the Korean-style sacrificial rite, the Rite to Royal Ancestors, was devised during the Joseon period.

2) The Components of the Rite to Confucius

a. Musical instruments (*ak*): Deungga (terrace ensemble) and heon-ga (courtyard ensemble)

In the Rite to Confucius, the terrace ensemble consists of the *pyeonjong* (bronze bell set), *pyeon-gyeong* (stone chime set), *teukjong* (single bronze bell), *teukgyeong* (single stone chime), *geum* (the Chinese zither *qin*), *seul* (zither with movable bridges), *so* (panpipes), *hun* (ocarina), *ji* (transverse flute), *yak* (end-blown flute), *jeok* (another end-blown flute), *jeolgo* (barrel drum), *bu* (clay vessel), *chuk* (wooden box with pestle), *eo* (tiger-shaped scraper), and *bak* (clapper). The courtyard ensemble consists of *pyeonjong*, *pyeon-gyeong*, *hun*, *ji*, *yak*, *jeok*, *nogo* (suspended drum set), *nodo* (pellet drum set), *jin-go* (barrel drum), *bu*, *chuk*, *eo*, and *bak*. The terrace ensemble is situated on a raised terrace near the shrine, and its music is quiet and delicate due to the use of stringed instruments (geum and seul) and singing. In contrast, the courtyard ensemble is situated at a lower

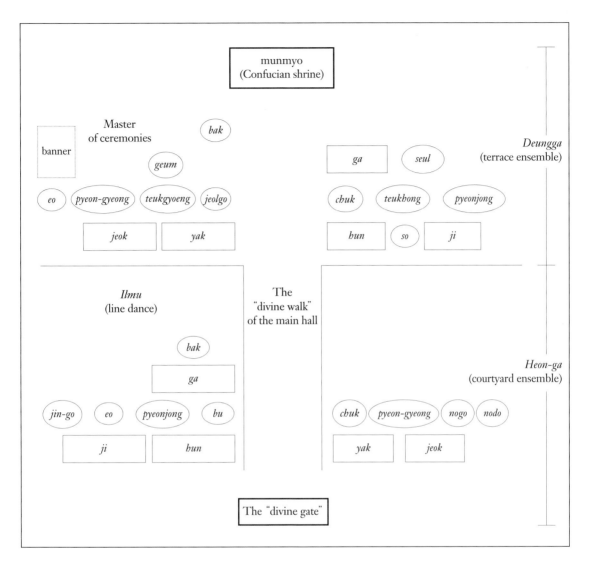

Within the figure:

munmyo
(Confucian shrine)

Master
of ceremonies

banner

bak

geum

Deungga
(terrace ensemble)

ga   *seul*

eo *pyeon-gyeong* *teukgyoeng* *jeolgo*

chuk   *teukhong*   *pyeonjong*

jeok   *yak*

hun   *so*   *ji*

Ilmu
(line dance)

The
"divine walk"
of the main hall

Heon-ga
(courtyard ensemble)

bak

ga

jin-go   *eo*   *pyeonjong*   *bu*

chuk *pyeon-gyeong* *nogo* *nodo*

ji   *hun*

yak   *jeok*

The "divine gate"

level in the courtyard, and its music is very loud as the ensemble mainly consists of large drums (jin-go, nogo and nodo) and wind instruments (hun, ji, yak, and jeok). Originally, it was strictly required that the court ritual music ensembles should include instruments made of all the eight materials (*pareum*), but today, the *saenghwang* (mouth organ), which represented the gourd category, is missing in the Rite to Confucius. The instrumentation of the terrace ensemble and courtyard ensemble in the Rite to Confucius has changed a number of times since this music was

Figure 24
Arrangement of the musicians in the Rite to Confucius.

Figure 25
A close-up view of the terrace ensemble in.

introduced during the Goryeo Dynasty (918-1392). The current version is the one transmitted from the Yi Wang-jik Aak-bu of the early 20th century.

B. Song (*ga*)

In the Rite to Confucius, the songs praise the great teachers who inspired humankind. As already mentioned, the subjects of veneration in the Rite to Confucius are four scholars: Confucius, Anzi, Xunzi, and Mengzi. Because of this, the Rite to Confucius originally included songs praising the virtues of each of these four men, but these have now been condensed into songs mainly for Confucius. As the rite originated in China, the songs also included songs borrowed from the Chinese version, but these were changed to some extent during the later Joseon period. In the sacrificial rites with music, the courtyard ensemble did not

Figure 26
Officiants in the Rite to
Confucius.

include singing. Thus, the court ritual music chapter of *Akhak gwebeom* (*Guide to the Study of Music*, 1493) lists songs only for the Jeonpye, Choheon, and Cheolbyeondu ceremonial procedures, which are accompanied by the terrace ensemble, and no song appears in other places such as the Yeongsin, Songsin, Aheon, and Jongheon procedures. However, in 1689 an official named Yi Bong-jing recommended the addition of songs to these prodedures, which was put into effect from the following year. At present, a total of six songs are sung.

In contrast to the Rite to Royal Ancestors, which uses a different verse form for each song, the songs of the Rite to Confucius conform to a Sino-Korean verse form in which four characters comprise a phrase and eight phrases form a verse. The songs have separate titles in which the Chinese character for "peace" (*an*) recurs like a refrain. Thus, "Eunganjiak" contains the meaning of "peace begins," "Myeonganjiak" of "peace shines brightly," "Seonganjiak" of "peace is accomplished," and "Oanji-ak" of "peace brings joy."

The aim of the Rite to Confucius is primarily to preach the importance of education and the idea that anyone can become a sage through learning. For this reason, one might expect that the songs would mention the ancient sage's high moral virtues in detail. Instead, however, the songs of the Rite to Confucius mainly pray for the harmonious union of people and god and for blessings upon all people through the correct performance of sacrificial rites in praise of virtue. This makes the content rather plain as a whole compared to the Rite to Royal Ancestors, which presents the achievements of past kings in detail.

The first song, "Eungan-jiak" for the Yeongsin procedure, welcomes Confucius as the outstanding teacher of everyone on earth and describes him descending to earth with the holy appearance of a saint. The second song, "Myeonganjiak" for the Jeonpye procedure, asks Confucius to accept the gifts and food that are offered to him with courtesy. The meaning of the Jeonpye can be recognized in the song text: "Gifts and sacrificial offerings are prepared thoroughly and the ceremony is performed with dignity; even if the sacrificial offering lacks something and is not fragrant, please hear our prayer." The third song, "Seonganjiak" for the Choheon procedure, originally had separate texts for Confucius, Anzi, Xunzi, and Mengzi. At present, however, only the song for Confucius is sung. It states that the great virtue of Confucius originated from heaven and therefore that the performance of sacrificial rites with music must never cease. The fourth song, "Seonganjiak," is sung twice, once in the Aheon procedure and once in the Jongheon procedure. It praises Confucius for leading people to live as they should, and completes the ceremony by offering him wine three times. The fifth song, "Oanjiak" for the Cheolbyeondu procedure, describes how a pure sacrificial offering brings people into harmony and pleases the gods. The text

Figure 27
Civil dance of the Rite to
Confucius.

Figure 28
Military dance of the Rite to
Confucius.

describes the procedures of the sacrificial rite quite specifically, mentioning that the ceremonial utensils *huijun* and *sangjun* are used for the wine
offering, that sacrificial offerings are placed in the wooden vessel du and
the basket byeon, and that "as the ceremony and music are wholly complete, the people are in harmony and the gods are pleased." The sixth
song, "Eungan-jiak" for the Songsin procedure, is the song for sending
the gods away after completing the sacrificial rite. It prays for the
departing god's abundant blessing upon the people after having accepted
with pleasure a rite offered with true devotion.

C. DANCE (*mu*): *Parilmu* (EIGHT-LINE DANCE)

Parilmu consists of the civil dance (*munmu*) and military dance (*mumu*)
presented at the Rite to Confucius. The civil dance begins in the
Yeongsin procedure and continues to the Jeonpye and Choheon procedures, whereas the military dance takes place in the Aheon and the
Jongheon procedures. All of the Ilmu dancers for the Rite to Confucius

wear a red overcoat, indigo waistband, and different hats for the civil and military dances. The hat for the civil dance is the jinhyeon-gwan that used to be worn by civil servants and Confucian scholars, whereas for the military dance a leather hat (*pibyeon*) is worn. In addition, for the civil dance, the dancers hold a flute (yak) in their left hand and a pheasant feather (jeok) in their right, whereas for the military dance, they hold a shield and an axe.

The dancing movements for the Rite to Confucius are very simple. In general, the Ilmu dances are simpler than other dances, but in its present form, the Ilmu dance for the Rite to Confucius is even simpler than that for the Rite to Royal Ancestors. The reason seems to be related to a change that occurred during the transitional period from the dynastic era to modern times. As the musical performance of the Rite to Confucius was remembered by a few court musicians, it was not difficult to transmit it to the next generation; but the same was not true of the dance. For the Rite to Confucius, large numbers of people were brought in and trained twice a year when the rite took place, but sometimes even this was not enough, and various people had to be recruited and taught simple movements to supply the dance for the sacrificial rite. As a last resort, the Sambangbae style of dance was devised, with movements maintaining the dignity of Parilmu but so radically simplified that they could be easily imitated by anyone. "*Sambangbae*" is a kind of bowing gesture whereby the dancers hold symbolic objects in their hands and move up and down while bending their upper bodies in three directions in turn. This kind of dance was continued in the Rite to Confucius until the 1970s. Today's version was standardized when the dancer Kim Yeongsuk reorganized the dance form after consulting senior members of the NCKTPA and a key text of Qing Dynasty China (1644-1911), *Ban-gung yeakseo*. In spring 1981, this version was officially approved as the dance for the Rite to Confucius. This was the dance performed in

1986 when the Rite to Confucius was designated Important Intangible Cultural Property No. 85.

3) Procedures and Musical Performance of the Rite to Confucius

In the Rite to Confucius, music is performed in the Yeongsin, Jeonpye, Choheon, Aheon, Jongheon, Cheolbyeondu, and Songsin ceremonial procedures. The dance, Ilmu, continues from the Yeongsin to the Jongheon procedures. The ceremonial procedures and the content of the musical performance from the Yeongsin to the Songsin ceremonies will now be described in detail.

Once the preparation for the sacrificial rite is completed, the Yeongsin ceremonial procedure begins. The master of the ceremony (*jimnye*) at the upper position orders the courtyard ensemble to perform "Eunganjiak" and "Yeolmunjimu," then the musical director (aksa) shouts "*Deuo!*," meaning "Lift up the flag," as a signal for the music to begin. The ensemble director (jipbak) sounds the clapper once and the mortar (chuk) is struck three times, followed by one stroke on the large drum (jin-go) and one more clap of the clapper. Only then do all the instruments join in performing the music for Yeongsin. The procedure for starting the music of the courtyard ensemble is always the same. For the Yeongsin procedure, the melody is played nine times in different keys: three times in C, twice in F, twice in A, and twice in A-flat. This follows the principle of "*yeongsin-guseong*": that is, the music is played nine times (nine being the perfect number) in the Yeongsin ceremony which welcomes the god in order to express sincere devotion. While the music is played, the priests stand motionless and reverently until the eighth repetition of the melody in A-flat, at which time they all bow four times. The pitch for each repetition of the melody is specified with terms referring

Figure 29
The altar-table prepared for
the Rite to Confucius.

to the 12 tones used in court ritual music: for instance, hwangjong is equivalent to the Western note C, *jungnyeo* to F, *namnyeo* to A, and *ichik* to A-flat. In effect, the same piece is transposed into different keys.

Once the ceremony and its accompanying music are completed, the musical director (aksa) gives the command for the music to stop by calling, "*Jio!*," meaning "Lower the flag." The ensemble director sounds the clapper three times in quick succession, the tiger-shaped scraper (*eo*) is also sounded three times, and the procedure comes to an end. The courtyard ensemble always concludes a musical performance in this way. The dancers, meanwhile, perform a civil dance.

With the completion of the Yeongsin ceremony, the Jeonpye ceremony begins. This time, the terrace ensemble plays "Myeonganjiak" and the dancers perform "Yeolmunjimu." The terrace ensemble plays the melody repeatedly in A throughout the ceremony. When the priest

Figure 30
Officiants preparing an
offering table.

appears after completing the ceremony, the musical performance is concluded with the sounding of the clapper (bak), single stone chime (teukgyeong), and scraper (eo) in rapid succession, even if the music has not been played right through to the end. The procedure for beginning the music is similar to that of the Yeongsin ceremony except that the single bronze bell (teukjong) is struck once after the first clapper stroke and once more before the second clapper stroke.

Next comes the Heonjak ceremonial procedure comprising the three wine offerings, Choheon, Aheon, and Jongheon. As in the Rite to Royal Ancestors, the Choheon procedure, where a written prayer is recited, is considered most important. For the Choheon ceremony, the terrace ensemble plays "Seonganjiak" in A and the dancers perform "Yeolmunjimu." It begins with an offering of a written prayer recited by the Choheon officiant. When the recitation is over, the musical performance begins with the sound of the clapper and three strokes on the barrel drum (jeolgo). Music and dance continue until the priest completes the ceremony at the shrine.

With the end of the Choheon ceremony, the performance of civil dance is finished and there is a procedure to prepare for the military dance. This procedure is described in the holgi for the sacrificial rite as "empty music" (gongak), meaning music performed without ceremony. To call music played in the absence of ritual "empty" shows how thoroughly jeryeak is centerd on ritual. In the past, there were separate dancers for the civil and military dances, and their entrance and exit took some time. Today, however, there is no exchange of dancers; the same dancers simply change their hats and symbolic objects to move from civil to military dance. This makes the procedure comparatively simple. The dancers take off the chinhyeon-gwan hats used for civil dance and replace them with the pibyeon-gwan symbolizing military dance. The flute and pheasant feather held in the hands for the civil dance are likewise replaced with the symbolic objects of military dance, the shield and axe.

When the preparation for military dance is completed, the Aheon and the Jongheon ceremonial prodedures commence. Here, the courtyard ensemble plays "Seonganjiak" in E and the military dance "Somujimu" is performed. Again, these are performed repeatedly until the ceremony is completed. Once the Jongheon is over, all the military dancers exit.

After the Heonjak ceremony, comes the Cheolbyeondu ceremony in which the ceremonial vessels are gathered up. Following the three offerings of wine (samheon), the worshipers burn additional incense and the choheon-gwan performs the Eumbok ceremony. Then, under the direction of the master of the ceremony (jimnye), the terrace ensemble plays "Oanjiak" in A. Finally, the Songsin ceremony for sending off the gods begins. For this, "Eungan-jiak" is performed by the courtyard ensemble. The music for the Songsin procedure uses its own melody in C that is different from the one used in Yeongsin, and this is called "Songsin hwangjonggung" (Songsin in C). After Songsin, there remains a written prayer and the burning of the entire offering of gifts, called Mangnyo. For this, "Eungan-jiak" in C is played once more by the courtyard ensemble to see the god off.

To summarize, the ceremonial procedures and musical content for the Rite to Confucius described heretofore are as follows:

Procedures and Music of the Rite to Confucius

Procedure	Title of music	Keys	Ensemble	Dance
Yeongsin	"Eungan-jiak"	C x 3	courtyard	civil: "Yeolmunjimu"
		F x 2		
		A x 2		
		A-flat x 2		
		(9 repetitions)		
Jeonpye	"Myeonganjiak"	A	terrace	civil: "Yeolmunjimu"
Choheon	"Seonganjiak"	A	terrace	civil: "Yeolmunjimu"
Gongak	"Seonganjiak"	E	courtyard	civil dancers exit; military dancers enter
Aheon	"Seonganjiak"	E	courtyard	military: "Somujimu"
Jongheon	"Seonganjiak"	E	courtyard	military: "Somujimu"
Cheolbyeondu	"Oanjiak"	A	terrace	military dancers exit
Songsin	"Eungan-jiak"	Songsin in C	courtyard	
Mangnyo	"Eungan-jiak"	Songsin in C	courtyard	

4) Musical Appreciation of the Rite to Confucius

Munmyo jeryeak is based upon a heptatonic scale, and its total musical range is a minor tenth (C to E-flat, the 12 chromatic notes of an octave plus 4 notes in the higher octave). Each musical piece in the Rite to

Confucius contains eight phrases, and each contains four Chinese characters of text each set to a single note in the syllabic style called *ilja ireum* (one character, one note). Moreover, each note of the melody is the same length, without rhythmic variation between long and short. The scale, musical range, phrasing and beat patterns of *Munmyo jeryeak* are all unique to Confucian ritual music and differ markedly from both traditional Korean music and from the non-ritual court music dangak that originated from China.

Name of the Twelve notes

Pitch	Korean	Chinese	Characters
C	hwangjong	huang-chung	黃鐘
C#	daeryeo	ta-lü	大呂
D	taeju	t'ai-ts'ou	太簇
C#	hyeopjong	chia-chung	夾鐘
E	goseon	ku-hsien	姑洗
F	jungnyeo	chung-lü	仲呂
F#	yubin	jui-pin	蕤賓
G	imjong	lin-chung	林鐘
G#	ichik	i-tse	夷則
A	namnyeo	nan-lü	南呂
A#	muyeok	wu-i	無射
B	eungjong	ying-chung	應鐘

Like the Rite to Royal Ancestors, the Rite to Confucius begins and ends with patterns unique to sacrificial music. But the beginning and ending patterns differ slightly between the terrace and the courtyard ensembles. When the courtyard ensemble begins, first the pellet drum (nodo) is shaken three times to create a fluttering sound. Then a pattern of three strokes on the mortar (chuk), one stroke on the suspended drum set (nogo), and one stroke on the barrel drum (jin-go) is repeated three times, and the clapper is sounded once, before the musical performance begins. The fluttering sound of the nodo, which is not used for the Rite to Royal Ancestors, creates a unique effect. When the music finishes, the ending is marked by playing three times three strokes on the nogo and jin-go, sounding the scraper (eo) three times, and sounding the clapper three or more times.

When the music of the terrace ensemble begins, the clapper is sounded followed by the single bronze bell. At the end, the clapper and bell are sounded at the same time, then the scraper is sounded three times. For the Choheonnye ceremony, after the reciting of a written prayer, the clapper and the jeolgo drum are sounded together three times before the music begins.

When the songs are sung, each note lasts about 5 to 7 seconds. According to descriptions of *Munmyo jeryeak* in the olden times from encyclopedias and such, each note lasted about 3 seconds, and from this we can tell that today's version has been slowed down somewhat. At the end of each note, the pitch is raised slightly, creating the feeling of a break in the melody. Here, the wind instruments—hun, ji, yak, and jeok—push the pitch up by about the interval of a second, ending each note as though drawing a curved line. The contrast between this bending of pitch and the fixed tones of the stone chime set (pyeon-gyeong) and bronze bell set (pyeonjong) creates a very mysterious feeling. Another characteristic of the courtyard ensemble is the beating of the clay vessel (bu) on the four beats of each phrase. This results in a very different feeling from the terrace ensemble, which plays without the accompaniment of the bu. When I listened carefully one time to the two ensembles—the courtyard ensemble with the bu playing on each note and the terrace ensemble without the bu—I noticed that the music played with the bu maintains the tempo steadily from beginning to end,

Hwangjong-gung (C)

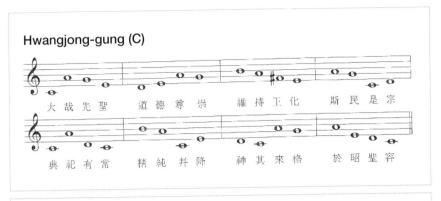

Namyeo-gung (A)

Goseon-gung (E)

Songsin hwangjong-gung (C)

Figure 31
Scores of "Eunganjiak" and
"Seonganjiak" from the
Rite to Contucius.

60

whereas in the absence of the bu the music becomes slower as it progresses. Thus, the function of the bu seems to be to regulate the tempo of the music.

The *Munyo jeryeak* performed today consists of six pieces. However, these pieces are not entirely different from each other. Five of them are actually the same tune transposed to different keys: C, F, A, A-flat, and E. In addition, there is different music in the key of C used for the Songsin ceremonial procedure that sends the gods off at the end. Excluding this Songsin music, the other five pieces differ in tonality but originated from the same piece. However, they sound quite different from each other. The reason lies in the rule that, in court ritual music, the melody must not move beyond the range of one octave plus four chromatic notes of the higher octave. For this reason, when the transposition of a melody results in notes that go beyond the boundary, these notes are played one octave higher or lower regardless of the melodic shape. Thus, the melodies contain frequent leaps. There were a greater number of pieces in the repertoire during the Joseon period than there are today. Besides the 11 pieces derived by transposing from C to all the other keys, there were Songsin pieces in C, E-flat, and G, and one additional piece. However, the rest of the pieces are no longer performed because the tradition of performing court ritual music has been discontinued except for the Rite to Confucius.

Thus, *Munmyo jeryeak* progresses smoothly without an expression of tension or release from the beginning to the end. This is because instrumental performances and vocal music move almost in unison, the beat is even, the notes are performed without dynamic variation, vibrato, or ornamentation, and the musical phrases are entirely regular. Such musical characteristics illustrate the principle of *dayuebiyi*, meaning "great music is invariably easy." (CD No.1, No.2)

5) Performance Tradition of the Rite to Confucius

During the Joseon Dynasty, the Eumagwon (Music Institute) was responsible for *Munmyo jeryeak*. Among the musicians, the aksaeng occupied a higher position than the akgong, who performed banquet music. The difference in social status among musicians appears to have been very strict. Although the Rite to Confucius is so simple that no high musicality or lengthy training was required, the mere fact of playing court ritual music elevated the status of musicians. This reflects the great importance that was attached to the court ritual music.

In the 20th century, however, the division disappeared and all students at the music institute learned both types of court music. In the early 20th century, the court music specialist school Yi Wang-jik Aak-bu Yangseongso taught the performing of the music after music theory had first been covered by the head teacher. During theory lessons, the history and playing techniques of the court musical instruments were taught. After completing the theoretical study, the students learned the music entirely through *gueum* (mnemonic syllables), then came the playing techniques for the pyeonjong, pyeon-gyeong, and jeolgo. When the students had become reasonably familiar with these, they progressed to learning the wind instruments. Although the musical pieces were very simple, it required great efforts to play music based on a heptatonic scale on instruments of such simple construction. On the wind instruments, one has to be able to produce semitones and quartertones from a limited number of finger holes.

Once the music had been mastered, an examination was held. First, knowledge of the music was tested through the mnemonic syllables, then the playing of pyeonjong, pyeon-gyeong, jeolgo, and ji were examined. The examination tested performance from memory of all the pieces that had been taught. However, rather than testing all six *gung* pieces, one had to draw lots from six pieces of rice paper, each marked with the name of one of the pieces: "Hwangjong-gung(C)," "Goseon-gung(E)," "Jungnyeo-gung(F)," "Ichik-gung(G#)," "Namnyeo-gung(A)," and "Songsin hwangjong-gung(O)." These were placed on the front of the teacher's desk. Each student then went forward and was required to perform the tune they had picked, by mnemonic syllables, either on pyeonjong, or on pyeon-gyeong. The examination assessment was either "pass" or "fail" and marked as 100 or 50, respectively. When the student who had failed retook an examination, the mark could rise to 70 or 80 points depending on the performance. The senior musician Seong Gyeong-nin(1911-2008), who was trained in court music in the early 20th century, recalled his life as a student:

The initial training for court musicians consisted of *Munmyo jeryeak* and *Jongmyo jeryeak* for the Royal Shrines of the Joseon Dynasty. Studies on the pyeonjong and pyeon-gyeong were the basic and fundamental subjects. Even in those days, each student had an individual desk. The lid could be lifted up and when put down it became a desk—it had an opening and shutting system. I drew a diagram of the 16 bells of the pyeonjong inside the desk lid, so that I could study the musical pieces any time. My senior Kim Cheon-heung(1909-2007) went one step further and wrote down the names of the 12 notes and 4 upper-octave notes of the pyeonjong, 16 letters in all, on his living room wall. He practiced every day by striking them with a wooden hammer. Without going to these lengths, it would have been difficult to memorize the whole court music repertoire, which is so extensive that it requires a long period of concentrated study without interruption.

Thanks to the musicians who made such great efforts to learn the ritual

Figure 32
Photographs of the Rite to
Confucius being performed
during the Japanese colo-
nial period (1910-1945).

music of the past and transmit the repertoire to the next generation, the
performance tradition of *Munmyo jeryeak* has been carried on to this day.

2. KOREAN-STYLE COURT RITUAL MUSIC: *JONGMYO JERYEAK*

1) The Rite to Royal Ancestors and Its Music

The Rite to Royal Ancestors is a ceremony venerating the preceding
kings of the Joseon Dynasty. At the Rite to Royal Ancestors, the king, as
the highest leader of the country, wore the highest ceremonial attire and
proceeded to the Jongmyo shrine together with his civil and military officials in a dignified and impressive street procession. Thereafter, the rite
was performed strictly according to rule in a reverent manner with food
and music in the highest style. The Rite to Royal Ancestors promoted
cohesion and order in the national community by providing a model of
filial piety to the people. It was the rite that affirmed the blood ties of the
royal family and clans and provided a foundation for communal life.

Among the Rites to Royal Ancestors of the Joseon period, the grand
ceremony with music, song and dance performances took place on spe-

cially designated days in the first, fourth, seventh and tenth lunar months and after celebrating the winter solstice each year. Besides these performances at Jeongjeon (Royal Audience Hall) of the Jongmyo shrine, the grand ceremony was also performed in the fourth and eighth months at the Yeongnyeong shrine. This means that during the Joseon period, the Rite to Royal Ancestors was performed a total of seven times a year.

After the decline of the Joseon Dynasty, the rite was transmitted as an ancestral rite of the Yi royal family during the Japanese colonial period. Amid the turbulent events of modern Korean history, such as the liberation from colonial rule in 1945 and the Korean War of 1950-1953, it could not escape discontinuation and change. Since 1969, it has been the rule to perform the Rite to Royal Ancestors with music and dance each year on the first Sunday in May by the solar calendar. For this, the Jeonju Lee Royal Family Members Foundation takes charge of the sacrificial rite, the NCKTPA provides the music, and students from the National Traditional Music High School perform the ceremonial dance. The rite can also be performed at other times and places by prior arrangement, for instance when there are large-scale national events such as the Olympics or the World Cup soccer tournament. Sometimes the sacrificial music is performed independently on stage as a musical performance or dance presentation. Certain pieces from the Rite to Royal Ancestors have become established as an important part of the traditional music repertoire.

SUPPLEMENTARY INFORMATION

JONGMYO: VENUE FOR THE RITE TO ROYAL ANCESTORS

The Rite to Royal Ancestors takes place at the Jongmyo shrine. Jongmyo is located in the Hunjeong-dong area of the Jongno district in

Figure 33
Jeongjeon, the main hall of
Jongmyo, the Royal
Ancestral Shrine.

Seoul, and was constructed together with Sajik (the national altar to the gods of land and grain) in 1395, shortly after the foundation of the Joseon Dynasty. When first built, the structure of Jongmyo consisted of the sinsil (shrine) where ancestral tablets were kept, which had five compartments, plus two side compartments on each side. In 1421, during King Sejong's reign, the Yeongnyeongjeon hall was built as a separate shrine behind the western part of Jongmyo. Later, during King Seonjo's reign, Jongmyo was destroyed in the Japanese invasion of 1592, but it was rebuilt during the reign of Gwanghae-gun (1608-1623). Since then, the building has been extended several times to accommodate the growing number of ancestral tablets, resulting in the long Jeongjeon and Yeongnyeongjeon buildings of today. Originally, the name Jongmyo referred to what is now called the Jeongjeon building, but today it refers to Jeongjeon and Yeongnyeongjeon together. The Jongmyo shrine is designated Historic Site No. 125, with Jeongjeon being designated

National Treasure No. 227, and Yeongnyeongjeon, Treasure No. 821.

At present, there are 19 cubicle-like shrines in the Jeongjeon building, covering the royal ancestors from the founder of the Joseon Dynasty to King Sunjong (r. 1907-1910), while the 16 cubicle shrines in the Yeongnyeongjeon house the ancestral tablets extending from Mokjo, the great-great-grandfather of the founder of the Joseon Dynasty, to the Crown Prince Uimin. In addition, 83 mortuary tablets of meritorious subjects who served the country during the Joseon Dynasty are enshrined at the Gongsindang.

2) The Components of the Rite to Royal Ancestors

The music for the Rite to Royal Ancestors, *Jongmyo jeryeak*, uses the deungga ensemble playing on the raised terrace and the heon-ga ensemble playing in the courtyard and accompanying the ceremonial dance.

Figure 34

Yeongnyeongjeon, an annex
of the Royal Ancestral
Shrine.

The dancers stand in a row at the foot of the west steps of Jongmyo.
Hereafter, the music and dance of *Jongmyo jeryeak* is discussed in detail.

A. MUSICAL INSTRUMENTS (*ak*): INSTRUMENTATION AND LAYOUT OF DEUNGGA AND HEON-GA

Jongmyo jeryeak employs a mixture of instruments from aak and from
non-ritual court music of both Tang Chinese (dangak) and indigenous
Korean (hyangak) origin. Because of its mixed instrumentation combining the dignity and symbolism of aak, the rich tone of dangak, and the
familiar sentiment of hyangak, *Jongmyo jeryeak* sounds quite different

from *Munmyo jeryeak*, which is performed solely on aak instruments. In today's *Jongmyo jeryeak*, both the deungga and heon-ga ensembles employ such instruments as the pyeonjong (bronze bell set), pyeongyeong (stone chime set), *banghyang* (iron chime set), chuk (wooden box with pestle), eo (tiger-shaped scraper), bak (clapper), *dangpiri* (oboe as used in dangak), *daegeum* (large transverse flute), *haegeum* (two-string fiddle), *ajaeng* (bowed zither), *janggu* (hourglass drum), *jing* (suspended gong), *taepyeongso* (shawm), jeolgo (barrel drum), and jin-go (large barrel drum). However, during the Joseon period there were additional musical instruments including the *gayageum* (zither with movable bridges), *geo-*

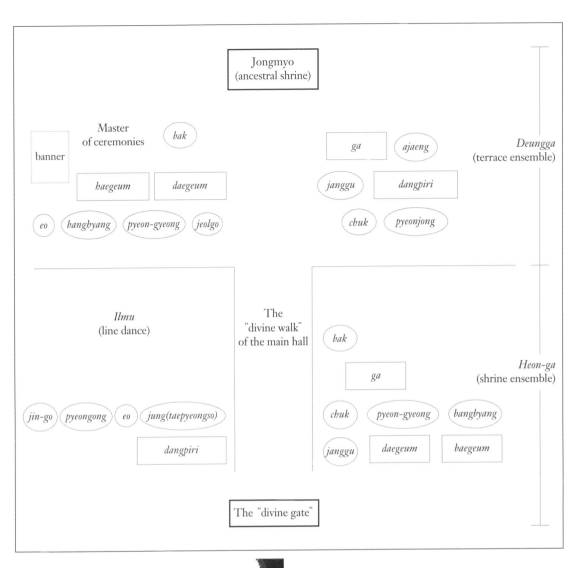

Jongmyo
(ancestral shrine)

Master
of ceremonies

banner

bak

ga   *ajaeng*

Deungga
(terrace ensemble)

haegeum   *daegeum*

janggu   *dangpiri*

eo   *banghyang*   *pyeon-gyeong*   *jeolgo*

chuk   *pyeonjong*

Ilmu
(line dance)

The
"divine walk"
of the main hall

bak

ga

Heon-ga
(shrine ensemble)

chuk   *pyeon-gyeong*   *banghyang*

jin-go   *pyeongong*   *eo*   *jung (taepyeongso)*

janggu   *daegeum*   *haegeum*

dangpiri

The "divine gate"

mun-go (zither with frets), wolgeum (lute with round body), *dangbipa* (lute as used in *dangak*), *hyangbipa* (lute as used in *hyangak*), *saeng* (mouth organ), *hwa* (small mouth organ), *wu* (large mouth organ), hun (ocarina), ji (transverse flute), *gwan* (pipe), *junggeum* (medium-sized transverse flute), *sogeum* (small bamboo flute), *dangjeok* (flute as used in *dangak*), *teukjong* (single bronze bell), teukgyeong (single stone chime), *gyobanggo* (suspended barrel drum), nogo (suspended drum set), and nodo (pellet drum set). The instrumentation and spatial plan of the terrace and courtyard ensembles are shown in Figure 35.

Figure 35
Arrangement of the musicians in the Rite to Royal Ancestors ensemble: the terrace and courtyard ensembles.

Left
Deungga, the terrace ensemble

Right
Heonga, the courtyard ensemble

B. SONG (*ga*) AND LYRICS

The songs of *Jongmyo jeryeak* express in detail the intention of offering a sacrificial ceremony, the stories of successive kings who devoted themselves to the people's wellbeing, their great contributions in maintaining the peace of the country, and prayers for the prosperity of their descendents' country.

> I, the king, came to the shrine of the ancestors
> to burn incense and perform a sacrificial rite without stinting,
> and welcome the gods with care.
> Please, gods, descend willingly
> and partake of the food I am offering,
> and I pray you to grant us abundant blessings again and again.

Thus, the song texts of *Jongmyo jeryeak* express the wish of the descendents to enjoy unlimited blessings through sacrificial rites performed with devotion. They contain a pledge that if the ancestor bestows a blessing, it will not be forgotten for a long time; a wish that the descendents may be so prosperous that they can flourish forever; and a request to ensure that the descendents who observe filial piety will live long lives full of happy events.

Another important aspect of the song texts is praise and admiration toward the ancestor to whom the sacrificial rite is offered. *Jongmyo jeryeak* consists of 22 short and independent musical pieces with subtitles, classified according to the subject of praise into "Botaepyeong-jiak" (Preserving the Peace) and "Jeongdaeeop-jiak" (Founding the Dynasty).

The 11 pieces of "Botaepyeong-jiak" ('Huimun,' 'Gimyeong,' 'Gwiin,' 'Hyeongga,' 'Jimnyeong,' 'Yunghwa,' 'Hyeonmi,' 'Yonggwang-jeongmyeong,' 'Junggwang,' 'Daeyu,' and 'Yeokseong') contain verses praising the civil achievements of the kings of many generations who helped preserve (*bo*) the peace (*taepyeong*) through their endeavors for the establishment and stability of the Joseon Dynasty. The 11 pieces of "Jeongdaeeop-jiak" ('Somu,' 'Dokgyeong,' 'Takjeong,' 'Seonwi,' 'Sinjeong,' 'Bunung,' 'Suneung,' 'Chongyu,' 'Jeongse,' 'Hyeokjeong,' and 'Yeonggwan') use poetic verses charged with an intrepid spirit to praise the military achievements of the four generations of founding kings and of the kings who have achieved (*jeong*) the great work (*daeeop*) of stabilizing the country since the foundation of the Joseon Dynasty by fighting foreign invaders. "When island barbarians attacked our borders and committed slaughter, the late kings became very angry and attacked the enemy's den. Like bird feathers in great flames, the raging waves subsided and our country's path became stabilized." Texts such as this one from 'Hyeokjeong' vividly describe the scene like a drama of victory.

Thus, the song texts of *Jongmyo jeryeak* clearly show the purpose of the rite: to pray for the everlasting prosperity of the royal family and the country by cherishing the memory of the royal ancestors with respect, devotion, ceremony and music, pure food and wine offerings. Furthermore, as described in the Confucian classic *Jungyong* (Doctrine of the Mean), "By offering the sacrificial ceremony at the Royal Shrine, the descendants are preserved." That is, the rite has an educational aim in encouraging the descendants to reflect on the lives of their ancestors and to govern the country on the model of the high aspirations of previous generations. The song texts of *Jongmyo jeryeak* are examined in detail here. (The complete texts are provided in Appendix I.).

a) Yeongsin – 'Huimun'

The song for welcoming the gods is titiled 'Huimun.' It prays for the virtue of the ancestors to come down to the descendants through a sacrificial rite that welcomes and entertains the spirits. The music of 'Huimun' is performed three times during the Rite to Royal Ancestors, in the Yeongsin, Jeonpye, and Choheon procedures. Although the melody is the same each time, the song texts differ, and also the tempo and ornamental details are very different. To distinguish them from the 'Huimun' of the Choheon procedure, the first two renditions are called 'Yeongsin huimun' and 'Jeonpye huimun,' respectively.

b) Jeonpye – 'Huimun'

The Jeonpye procedure expresses the wish that the gods will accept the offerings prepared with true devotion. The song texts for offering gifts are sung to the 'Huimun' melody as it appears in the Choheon procedure.

c) Jinchan – 'Pungan-jiak'

'Pungan-jiak' in the Jinchan procedure is structured in a fixed verse form of six phrases, each containing four characters, and its content describes the offering of food to the gods.

d) Choheon – "Botaepyeong-jiak"

The 11 pieces of "Botaepyeong" accompany the Choheon procedure in which the first offering of wine is made to the ancestors. Among the

11 pieces, the first piece 'Huimun' is the prelude to "Botaepyeong-jiak," and the 11th piece "Yeokseong" is a concluding piece. Thus, the main content of praising the ancestors is expressed in the other nine pieces. The same structure, with nine pieces between the prelude and the concluding piece, is also used in "Jeongdaeeop-jiak." The reason for structuring the main content of the sacrificial rite music in nine pieces is believed to reflect the significance attached to the number nine.

The first piece, 'Huimun,' expresses thanks for the past kings' reign over Joseon with a splendid and beautiful culture. The title 'Huimun' derives from two characters in the song texts, the '*hui*' of *huiun* and the '*mun*' of *munchi*.

The second piece, 'Gimyeong,' is a song of praise for Yi Ansa (Mokjo), great-great-grandfather of the founder of the Joseon Dynasty, Yi Seonggye (King Taejo). It celebrates Mokjo's move to Gyeongheung in the northeastern region and the people's rallying around him, which contributed to the establishment of the dynasty. The title 'Gimyeong' is derived from the concluding phrase, '*giayeongmyeong*.'

The third piece, 'Gwiin,' is a praise song for Yi Haeng-ni (Ikjo), the great-grandfather of King Taejo. It describes how, when Ikjo returned from Jeokdo to live in Deogwon, the people following him were as numerous as a market crowd. The title 'Gwiin' comes from the phrase '*yuinjigwi*.'

The fourth piece, 'Hyeongga,' tells how Ikjo and Dojo, the grandfather of King Taejo, served the Goryeo king, who favored them and commended them for their good deeds. The song explains how the trust built by the ancestors later became the foundation for the establishment of the Joseon Dynasty.

The fifth piece, 'Jimnyeong,' praises the meritorious deeds of Hwanjo(1315-1360), the father of King Taejo, who followed King Gongmin's order at the end of the Goryeo Dynasty, drove out the influ-

ence of the Gi family of Ssangseongchonggwanbu ssangseong comman-
dery in Hamgyeong prulince and contributed to the expansion of territory in the northeastern region. The song indicates that Hwanjo earned
the people's trust through his peaceful rule over the region, thus secur-
ing an indispensable foundation for the establishment of the Joseon
Dynasty. The title 'Jimnyeong' comes from the fifth phrase of the song
text, 'songhwajimnyeong.'

The sixth piece, 'Yunghwa,' praises the virtues of the founder of the
Joseon Dynasty, King Taejo(1335-1408), singing of the innumerable fol-
lowers from the whole country and overseas who gave him their enthu-
siastic support. The title 'Yunghwa' derives from the fourth phrase of the
Sino-Korean verse, 'sinhwayungheup.'

The seventh piece, 'Hyeonmi,' praises King Taejong's(1367-1422)
virtue in yielding the throne to his brother Jeongjong(1357-1419)
regardless of the people's requests for him to become the Crown Prince
after he suppressed Jeong Do-jeon's(1342-1398) revolt. The title
'Hyeonmi' is derived from the fourth phrase, 'donyanghyeonmideok.'

The eighth piece, 'Yonggwangjeongmyeong,' combines what were
originally two independent pieces, 'Yonggwang' and 'Jeongmyeong.'
'Yonggwang' narrates the events surrounding King Taejong's accession
to the throne, the anger it caused in Ming Dynasty China(1368-1644),
which considered it unjustifiable, and the resolution of the situation
through King Taejong's visit to China. 'Jeongmyeong' praises Queen
Won-gyeong(1365-1420) who assisted King Taejong when Jeong Do-
jeon's(1342-1398) revolt started. The title 'Yonggwang' originated from
'hyeokjaeyonggwang' and the title 'Jeongmyeong' originated from 'uiyeo-
jeongmyeong.'

The ninth piece, 'Junggwang,' uses a Chinese verse form of eight
phrases, each containing four characters. It praises the achievements of
the ancestors who fought against the Japanese Invasion of Korea in 1592

and restored peace to the Royal Ancestral Shrine and the state. This piece was added in the third year of King Injo's reign, 1625. The title is derived from the second phrase, '*jundeokjunggwang*.'

The tenth piece, 'Daeyu,' summarizes a theme that runs through the whole of "Botaepyeong-jiak," describing how the civil achievements of the ancestors contributed to the establishment of ceremony and music and a peaceful reign. The title 'Daeyu' comes from the fourth phrase, '*daeyuhahwanghwang*.'

The 11th piece 'Yeokseong,' concludes the "Botaepyeong-jiak" suite that is performed during the Choheon procedure of the Rite to Royal Ancestors. While it is played by the terrace ensemble, the ceremonial dancers perform a civil dance and then exit. Thus, the piece is also called 'Inchuljang,' or 'exit music.' The song describes how the ancestors' merit and virtue should spread widely as the Choheon procedure is completed with the accompaniment of musical performance in the proper style.

e) Aheon, Jongheon – "Jeongdaeeop-jiak"

"Jeongdaeeop-jiak" is performed in the Aheon and Jongheon procedures. "Jeongdaeeop-jiak" also consists of 11 pieces in all, with the first piece 'Somu' and the 11th piece 'Yeonggwan' forming the prelude and concluding piece and the other nine pieces praising the ancestors' military achievements.

The first piece of "Jeongdaeeop-jiak" is 'Somu.' While this piece is performed, the dancers for the military dance enter; thus, 'Somu' is also known as 'Inipjang,' or 'entrance music.' The song summarizes the overall theme of "Jeongdaeeop-jiak," expressing thanks for heaven's care bestowed on the ancestors that enabled the success in war and the accumulation of distinguished military accomplishments through the generations. The title "Somu" derives from the second phrase, '*kyesesoseongmu*.'

The second piece, 'Dokgyeong,' sings the praises of Mokjo, the great-

great-grandfather of King Taejo, for his military achievements. In phrases of four characters, the song describes Mokjo's conquest of the northern region and his peaceful reign over the people that led to the establishment of the Joseon Dynasty. The title 'Dokgyeong' comes from the third phrase, '*hyuldokgigyeong*.'

The third piece, 'Takjeong,' praises Dojo's outstanding military achievements and Hwanjo's subjugation of the rebellion that took place in Ssangseong. Yi Ja-chun (Hwanjo), the father of King Taejo, followed King Gongmin's order at the end of the Goryeo Dynasty to drive out the influence of the Gi family of Ssangseongchonggwanbu, contributing to the expansion of territory in the northeastern region and hence to the foundation of the Joseon Dynasty. The title 'Takjeong' derives from the fourth phrase, '*utakjeong*.'

The fourth piece, 'Seonwi,' praises the glorious achievement of King Taejo in defeating the attack of the Red Turban Bandits (Honggeon-jeok). The song expresses vividly the outstanding military contribution that Taejo made against the foreign enemy's invasion, which had combined with other causes to throw the country into disorder. The title, 'Seonwi,' comes from the 11th phrase, '*jaeseoncheonwi*.'

The fifth piece, 'Sinjeong,' praises King Taejo's victories against both the Red Turban Bandits and the Japanese pirate raiders. Throughout this song, the indomitable courage of King Taejo in suppressing the enemy at a stroke is expressed in images such as that of a tiger being felled by an axe, or the splitting of bamboo. The title "Sinjeong" is derived from the 12th and 13th phrases of the text, '*gijeongmu sinjii*,' by taking one character from each.

The sixth piece, 'Bunung,' also praises Taejo's intrepid military achievements. It expresses the hope that once the enemy is completely mown down and subjugated, peace will endure in the future. The title 'Bunung' comes from the first phrase, '*aungabun*.'

The seventh piece, 'Suneung,' signifies "follow (*sun*) the way of Heaven and obey (*eung*) the way of humanity." This indicates that King Taejo's plot for establishing the Joseon Dynasty by withdrawing his troops at Wihwado Island was in accord with the will of both heaven and the people. The final phrase of 'Suneung,' '*cheoninhyeopchan*,' can be described as the kernel of the song.

The eighth song, 'Chongsu,' emphasizes that King Taejo's establishment of the dynasty and of himself as king was the heavenly wish. It describes how, when Taejo withdrew his troops at Wihwado Island, providential help appeared in many forms, and the people welcomed his venture. The title 'Chongsu' comes from the fifth phrase, '*hyeachongsu*,' which implies the meaning of anticipating love and peace.

The ninth piece, 'Jeongse,' sings that when Jeong Mong-ju (Poeun), the last loyal subject of the Goryeo Dynasty, tried to oppose King Taejo's plot of establishing a new dynasty, Yi Bang-won (the future King Taejong) discovered the secret and killed him. This song pays tribute to the resolution of the conflict and the bringing forth of peace. The title

'Jeongse' derives from the third to sixth phrases, '*sinmojeong seijeong.*'

The tenth piece, 'Hyeokjeong,' praises King Taejo's military achievements. Like the songs discussed earlier, it describes the scene of attacking foreign invaders very vividly. The two characters of the title are taken from the third and fourth phrases of the text, '*wonhyeokkano wonjeongaryeo.*'

The 11th piece, 'Yeonggwan,' announces the completion of the sacrificial rite accompanied by the songs and dances of "Jeongdaeeop-jiak." The title 'Yeonggwan' comes from the concluding phrase, '*yeonggwangwolseong.*' This song embodies the image of sacrificial music that leaves a lingering impression through its dignified and serene melody.

f) Cheolbyeondu – "Eungan-jiak"

Cheolbyeondu is the procedure of gathering up the ceremonial utensils used in the sacrificial rite. Therefore, its song text mentions the food and utensils used in sacrifices, and states that as the food offered on the sacrificial table emits fragrance, one can tell that the ancestral spirits have visited. The melody is the same as that of "Pungan-jiak" in the Jinchan procedure, but the song texts differ.

g) Songsin – "Heungan-jiak"

"Heungan-jiak" is the music of the Songsin procedure, in which the spirits are sent away. Its song text reads, "As the sacrificial rite was held according to the rules / Were you spirits feeling comfortable and delighted? / Before going any further on your way / Turn your head to look at us once more. / Riding on clouds that look like a rainbow banner / You depart into the distance." This song intimately describes the feeling of sadness at parting with the ancestral spirits and the scene of the spirits departing. The melody and the structure are the same as "Pungan-jiak" in the Jinchan procedure.

The song texts of *Jongmyo jeryeak* went through some changes in content during the Japanese colonial period. The colonial government downgraded the status of the Imperial Household of the Joseon Dynasty to the Yi Royal Family and curtailed the scale of the Rite to Royal Ancestors from that of the state to a family sacrificial rite. In the process, from the song texts of *Jongmyo jeryeak*, the phrases that either symbolized the state or praised the distinguished services against the Japanese invasions in history were all changed.

This situation continued for a considerable period even after Korea's liberation from Japanese colonial rule. Although scholars restored the ceremony to its original version after liberation, it was not until the 1980s that musicians began to sing the corrected song texts. The reasons for this can be interpreted in a number of ways. First of all, in the chaotic political situation between Liberation and the Korean War, there was little concern for the Rite to Royal Ancestors. Until the late 1960s, the rite was discontinued, and the music, song, and dance of *Jongmyo jeryeak* was never performed completely from beginning to end in the ritual context. Since no sacrificial rite fully equipped with musical accompaniment was ever presented, nobody paid attention to the meaning of the song texts. During this hiatus, the Rite to Royal Ancestors was transmitted only as "music." Therefore, musicians had to grapple with the problem of how to sing it, without understanding the exact meaning of the song texts written in Chinese characters. As a result, no attention was given to the change that occurred in the song texts during the Japanese colonial period until the revised version began to be sung in the 1980s.

This became an object of public interest in the early 2000s when several scholars, who were concerned with the modern transmission of traditional music, pointed out the distortion of the historical accounts by the Japanese colonial government. This then became a sensitive issue. The reason that the song texts of the Rite to Royal Ancestors went through the aforementioned changes lay in the fact that this was sacrificial music symbolizing the state. The reason that it took a long time to correct the song texts, which had been intentionally revised by the Japanese colonial government, was probably because the Rite to Royal Ancestors was not of interest to the public at the time.

h) Musical Images Manifested in the Song Texts of the Rite to Royal Ancestors

In these song texts, it is interesting to find phrases that refer to the musical elements of *Jongmyo jeryeak*, such as "*jangjang*," "*eumeum*," and "*hwanghwang*." "*Jangjang*" is an onomatopoeic word for the effect of the pyeonjong and pyeon-gyeong brightly resonating in harmony. "*Eumeum*" refers to the peaceful resonating sounds from the bells and drums, and "*hwanghwang*" is an expression that refers to the majestic atmosphere created by a combination of bell and drum sounds. The phrase "*wiwitata*," as in "that grand appearance is *wiwitata* like the mountains and sea" from "Jeongdaeeop-jiak," originated from a poetic phrase in the *Shih Ching* (*Book of Songs*). Referring to the appearance of a mind and attitude that are in accord and serene (*ongyongjadeuk*), this phrase evokes the whole image of "Jeongdaeeop-jiak." "Jeongdaeeop" also contains the lines, "Ah, ah, our ancestors had military merits generation after generation / How can we adequately express their royal virtues and great achievements? / There is order in dance and law in movement / Thus ending the music slowly and with dignity." This reveals the fact that "Jeongdaeeop-jiak," which praises the dynasty's military achievements, is music for a king who governs his people to enjoy a settled life through his relaxed, dignified, peaceful, and calm leadership of troops.

c. Mu – Ilmu (ceremonial dance)

When performing a ceremonial dance in the Rite to Royal Ancestors, all the dancers wear red overcoats and blue waistbands. As for the shoes, they wear a pair of black boots coming up to the ankles, and on the head they wear a hat called *bokdu*. The hand-held props are called *uimul*, meaning "ceremonial objects." For a civil dance, the dancers hold the yak, a kind of flute, in their left hand, and the jeok, a pheasant feather, in their right. The yak has three finger holes, implying that all kinds of sounds are made in harmony through the three holes. The jeok is made of a wooden stick measuring about one *ja* (33cm) long, with a pheasant feather tied to it and elaborate decorative knot-work hanging down. All of these symbolize peace and order.

During the civil dance, the dancers perform while making rhythmic sounds by striking the yak and jeok against each other. The dance movements change slowly, without intense variation such as sitting and rising or whirling round and round. The dancers, standing in one position, continue to repeat slow movements such as lifting and lowering both of their arms, bending or stretching the upper half of their body, or turning slowly to the right or left. The movements look simple but pious.

The civil dance is performed from the Yeongsin to the Choheon procedures and is accompanied by "Pungan-jiak" during the Jinchan procedure and by "Botaepyeong-jiak" during the rest of the procedures. The military dance is performed with the front four rows of dancers holding a sword and the back four rows a spear. When the music begins, the military dancers repeat comparatively simple movements while making themselves ready to start by putting their hands together in front of their chests. The movement includes turning the body first to the left and then to the right, while opening both hands and lifting and lowering the right hand to and from the top of the head. From these military dance movements performed to the gallant melodies of "Jeongdaeeop-jiak," we can get a glimpse of military majesty.

The movements of the civil and military dances are sometimes explained on the yin-yang principle. For example, when starting a civil dance the body is lowered before continuing to the next movement, whereas the military dance must begin with the posture of lifting one's head up and then continuing to the next movement. This implies that the civil dance has a quality of yin, expressing humility and retreat, whereas the military dance has a quality of yang, showing an energetic spirit through upward movement. The fact that all dance movements begin with a gesture of bringing together both hands on the chest and end with *haphyung* (open arms) follows the same principle as that of the music, that the ending note should be the same as the starting note.

The Ilmu is considered as a dance form that expresses the reverence and modesty of humankind through gentle movements in perfect harmony with music. The ceremonial dance still maintains the image portrayed in the classic text *Akki*, which states, "Ak is the dance movement accompanied by *gancheok* and *umo*. Gancheok is a military dance and umo is a civil dance."

Figure 37
Illustration of the Ilmu ceremonial dance on the dance score *Siyong mubo*.

The ceremonial dance of the Rite to Royal Ancestors was reconstructed and performed again during King Sejong's reign through research carried out on music and dance of ancient China. Although the external structure is similar to the ceremonial dance for aak, it came to possess unique characteristics. King Sejong made every possible effort to devise a dance that would symbolize civil virtue and military achievements in order to extol the contributions that the past kings had made for the establishment and stabilization of the country. Originally, this dance was created for royal banquets, but from the 10th year of King Sejo's reign (1464) it was performed at both banquets and sacrificial rites. For this reason, when the same dance was performed for banquets and sacrificial rites for some time, it came to be transmitted with differences in the dancers, gender, costumes, and props. For the sacrificial rites, male dancers wore a jinhyeon-gwan on the head and a blue overcoat for a civil dance and a pibyeon headdress for a military dance, while for banquets, pretty female dancers performed with colorful ornaments.

"Jeongdaeeop-jiak," in particular, was markedly different. First of all, 35 attendants called *uimuljabi* stood in a row, adding dignity by holding musical instruments and ceremonial props such as the *gak* (conch shell), *duk*, *go* (drum), *geum* (gong), *gi* (flag), *ra* (trumpet), *daego* (large drum), and *daegeum* (large gong), plus flags representing *jujak* (red phoenix), *cheongnyong* (blue dragon), *hwangnyong* (yellow dragon), *baekho* (white tiger), and *hyeonmu* (black tortoise). When dancing, ceremonial props, such as a sword, spear, or bow and arrow, were employed, creating a military dance that was much more varied and splendid than the ceremonial dance of aak. In the "Jeongdaeeopjimu" military dance, the use of flags in five colors showing the animal deities, of percussion musical instruments that had been used in military parades since the Goryeo Dynasty, and of the 35 attendants in a line holding ceremonial props in addition to the dancers for *yugilmu* (six-line dance), all can be considered as creative expressions of the Joseon Dynasty that are different from those of China.

However, the presentation of this "Jeongdaeeopjimu" was changed around the time of the Japanese Invasion of Korea in 1592 and the Manchu Invasion of 1636. Originally, it had an alternating format in which, as the rite progressed, the dancers for "Botaepyeong-jiak" would exit before the entrance of the dancers for "Jeongdaeeopjimu." Later, it changed into a format where the dancers simply changed their props without the entrance and exit procedures. Furthermore, "Jeongdaeopji-ak" was originally performed as a representational dance in battle array, but it later changed to the plain format of today in which the *uimuljabi* (the attendants holding the ceremonial props) were eliminated and the dancers wore the same costumes as for the civil dance. This may have resulted from the fact that its use in banquets became reduced, and as it was performed mainly for the sacrificial rites, it came to be influenced by the simpler ceremonial music and dance.

The dance for the Rite to Royal Ancestors as performed at the state ceremony was transmitted without departing too much from the framework set out in a dance score titled the "Siyong mubo" which recorded the dancers' movements. However, in the transmission processes of dance there were often times when the ceremonial dance was discontinued, especially during wars or when the country was in a crisis, due to the large number of people required to perform it. For this reason, throughout its history one can find complaints that the dance "did not correspond to the original" or "was not in accord with any of the rules." Today's dance for the Rite to Royal Ancestors is based upon the version transmitted by the late-19th-century court musicians at the Yi Wang-jik Aak-bu, and since 1961 it has been preserved and transmitted as an Important Intangible Cultural Property of the country.

3) Procedures and Musical Performance of the Rite to Royal Ancestors

The performance of *Jongmyo jeryeak* is described in detail here. Once the Yeongsin procedure begins, the steward in charge of the ceremony gives an order in a unique recitation style, saying, "The terrace ensemble begins "Botaepyeong-jiak" and the dancers perform "Botaepyeongjimu"; the courtyard ensemble plays "Botaepyeong-jiak" and the dancers perform "Botaepyeongjimu." Then the steward in charge of the music shouts briefly, "Raise the flags." On this signal, the terrace ensemble plays "Yeongsin huimun" to welcome the spirits. "Yeongsin huimun" is repeated nine times according to the principle of "*yeongsin guseong*" (welcoming with a formation of nine). Despite its profound meaning, in theory, actually playing the same piece nine times must not have been very effective in practice. Furthermore, on a snowy winter's day or a humid midsummer night swarming with mosquitoes, performing the same piece nine times in the sacrificial rite must have been such a difficult task that the performers were desperate to end the rite as quickly as possible.

Perhaps that's why, according to a senior instrumentalist who performed in the sacrificial rite tradition at the end of the Joseon Dynasty, the nine repetitions of "Yeongsin huimun" were played at a rapid tempo, as if the musicians were dashing through the music to complete the required number of repetitions quickly. The musicians would justify this by saying that there was no harm in playing the nine repetitions of "Yeongsin huimun" at a fast tempo because it signified, "Oh, spirits! Please come without delay!" This anecdote vividly conveys the feelings of the musicians who had to play the same piece nine times in a row. It also makes us realize how many different factors can cause music to change with the passage of time.

After being played so rapidly in the Yeongsin procedure, "Huimun" is played several times slower in the Jeonpye procedure. The reason for the slower performance might have had something to do with the need to accompany the entire ceremonial procedure of presenting sacrificial offerings, but perhaps more importantly it was a way of introducing musical variety through a change in tempo. It may also have served the purpose of expressing maximum reverence during the presentation of ceremonial offerings.

For the Jinchan procedure of offering food on the ceremonial table, the Chinese-style music "Pungan-jiak" is played without ceremonial dance.

For the Choheon procedure, the terrace ensemble plays "Botaepyeong-jiak" accompanied with a civil dance, whereas for the Aheon and the Jongheon procedures the courtyard ensemble plays "Jeongdaeeop-jiak" accompanied with a military dance. The Aheon procedure begins with *jin-go siptong*, in which a large drum called jin-go is struck ten times, before "Somu," the first piece of "Jeongdaeopjiak," is performed. In the Jongheon procedure, the music begins with three strokes on the jin-go.

When Jongheon is completed, the Eumbok procedure is performed without music, then the procedure of Cheolbyeondu (gathering in the ceremonial utensils) is accompanied by the terrace ensemble's performance of "Onganjiak" without dance. Following this, a priest and all other participants bow four times and the rite comes to an end with the Songsin procedure of sending off the spirits accompanied by the performance of "Heungan-jiak."

To summarize, the following table illustrates the procedures of the Rite to Royal Ancestors comprising the Yeongsin, Jeonpye, Jinchan, Heonjak (Choheon, Aheon, and Jongheon), Eumbok, Cheolbyeondu, Songsin, and Mangnyo ceremonies.

Procedure	Title of music	Ensemble	Dance
Yeongsin	"Huimun" ("Yeongsin huimun")	courtyard	"Botaepyeongjimu"
Jeonpye	"Huimun" ("Jeonpye huimun")	terrace	"Botaepyeongjimu"
Jinchan	"Pungan-jiak"	courtyard	
Heonjak Choheon	"Botaepyeong-jiak"	terrace	"Botaepyeongjimu"
Aheon	"Jeongdaeeop-jiak"	courtyard	"Jeongdaeeopjimu"
Jongheon	"Jeongdaeeop-jiak"	courtyard	"Jeongdaeeopjimu"
Eumbok	(no music)		
Cheolbyeondu	"Pungan-jiak"	terrace	
Mangnyo	"Pungan-jiak"	courtyard	

4) Musical Appreciation of the Rite to Royal Ancestors

A. Percussion musical phrases played at the beginning and ending of a performance

In the music for sacrificial rites, there is a standard introductory pattern played on the chuk (mortar) and drums before the main melody starts, and a concluding pattern played at the end. These are called *akjak* and *akji*, respectively. In *Jongmyo jeryeak*, after the musical conductor gives one loud clap on the bak (clapper), the chuk player strikes the instrument as if pounding grain in a wooden mortar, in a pattern repeated three times: "*kung kungkung, kung kungkung, kung kungkung.*" Next, the jeolgo (barrel drum) is struck three times, followed by one more clap of the clapper. This very distinctive pattern is described as "*gyeokbak-ilseong gochuksamseong gyeokgoiltong,*" which means "sound the clapper once by striking it once; make the chuk sound three times for each stroke; and make the drum sound once per stroke." What is the reason for playing the percussion instruments before introducing the main piece? Having been passed down for a long time as a tradition of Confucian ritual, it could have many symbolic meanings. But, looking at it from the listener's point of view, it can be considered as a musical device creating a very special effect that would attract people's attention to the music.

This introductory pattern is called akjak, meaning "to begin the music." There is also a concluding pattern called akji that completes the music. To end the musical performance, the steward would first shout "*Jio!*" The word "*jio*" is the opposite of "*deulla*" (to lift), thus implying that the flag is lowered. Then the clapper and drum are struck: "ttak ttak ttak, kung kung kung," and instead of the chuk symbolizing the beginning, the eo (tiger-shaped scraper) symbolizing the ending is struck with a sound like "taktaktak tageureureureu, taktaktak tageureureureu, taktaktak tageureureureu," thus bringing the whole performance to an end.

Actually, the introductory pattern is varied slightly depending on the piece. In *Munmyo jeryeak*, the introductory pattern contains a sound like "hududududuk, hududududuk," which does not appear in *Jongmyo jeryeak*. The sound comes from the nodo, a pellet drum which is not played with sticks but is shaken so that the heads are struck by pellets on the ends of strings attached to the body of the drum. In *Jongmyo jeryeak*, when a piece is played by the courtyard ensemble, it uses the jin-go (large barrel drum) in place of the *jeolgo* of the terrace ensemble. In this case, there are two ways of starting the music: *jin-go siptong*, by striking the jin-go 10 times, and *jin-go samtong*, by striking it 3 times. As the jin-go is very large even compared to other barrel drums, it creates a majestic sound. The reason for employing the jin-go at the beginning is that the piece performed symbolizes the military aspect of the dance.

Just as there are several ways of varying the introductory pattern of a piece, there are also differences in the concluding patterns. In general, to end a piece, the clapper, jeolgo, and jin-go are struck three times and the scraping sound of the eo concludes the music. However, the ending of the Jongheon procedure is distinctive in that the music is concluded with three strokes on the clapper and three on the jin-go, followed by the eo and the metallic percussion instrument jing making a sound like "dangdang, dangdang, dangdang, dangdang, dang, dang." This is described as "*daegeum sipcha*" (10 strokes on the large gong). The lingering sound of the jing seems to create a special grandeur.

B. Instrumentation and Tone Color

Jongmyo jeryeak combines songs, dances, and performance on various musical instruments in harmonious unity. Since the Rite to Royal Ancestors is a festival praying for national prosperity and the welfare of the people through the king's filial piety protected by the grace of heaven, its ultimate aim is to promote harmony between "heaven, the earth, and people" (*cheonjiin*). Therefore, the procedure of the entire rite and its content, such as the musical performance, dance, food and costumes, are organized according to the balance of these three elements. It is thought that the music performed at the Sangwoldae of the royal audience chamber symbolized heaven, while that performed at the Hawoldae symbolized the earth, and the ceremonial dance symbolized human beings.

The most striking characteristic of *Jongmyo jeryeak* is its unique blend of tone colors. If you put on a CD containing various kinds of Korean court music and selected the tracks at random to compare the sound of each piece, you would notice that the sound of *Jongmyo jeryeak* differs markedly from that of "Sujecheon, "Boheoja," or "Gwanak yeongsan-hoesang."

The banghyang, pyeon-gyeong, and pyeonjong play fixed notes whereas the haegeum, ajaeng, daegeum, dangpiri, and sogeum play the tunes with various ornamentation that do not appear in the score. At the same time, the pyeon-gyeong, pyeonjong, and banghyang play a succession of detached notes because their sound decays rapidly while the notes are long. The sogeum plays an octave higher than the other wind instruments with much more elaborate ornamention. The combination of these contrasting timbres creates a unique harmony of sounds that is beyond description.

In particular, the dangpiri is used for *Jongmyo jeryeak* because its volume is louder and its tone color darker than the hyangpiri. When the dangpiri plays the main melody in contrast with the daegeum and sogeum parts, the effect is overwhelming. The playing technique of the dangpiri, which draws out a single note at length before bursting into a vigorous ornamental melody, is an important element that imparts great vitality to *Jongmyo jeryeak* while forming an exquisite contrast to the other wind instruments.

C. VOCALIZATION AND PRONUNCIATION OF THE SONG TEXTS

Another important element in defining the image of *Jongmyo jeryeak* is the songs. The main song texts of *Jongmyo jeryeak* are lyrics written in Chinese verse. One of their most striking features is the use of interpolated vowels such as "*ae*" or "*heu*" inserted into the text. These vowels mainly appear at the end of a line, but they can also appear in unexpected places. These interpolated vowels are different from those of *pansori* (musical story-telling) or *jeongga* (lyric songs). In pansori, *gagok* (lyric songs), or *sijo* (three-line poem) singing, when a note is extended in duration, the vowel is relaxed: for instance, *dongchang-i* (a window to the east) would be sung as "dongchaaaeuang." Also, when a melodic pattern ascends from a low note to a high note and descends again, the relaxing of the vowel appears generally in the singing of the high notes. However, the songs of *Jongmyo jeryeak* are different. A sound that bears no relation to the text may be inserted at the end of a musical phrase, or extra vowels may be interpolated into the beginning or middle part of the phrase. This is an important element that gives a different taste to *Jongmyo jeryeak*. For example, in "Huimun," the Chinese song text "*sedeokgyeahu ososanghyeongseong*" is broken up as "*sedeo—gye-a—hu—ae— /oso—sang—o—hyeo—o-ae—seo-o ae—*," with added vowels such as "*ae*" that bear no relation to the original lyrics.

This singing practice of adding or changing vowels can only be found in Jongmyo jeryeak, and is thus a unique characteristic of the genre. The voice is used in a natural way without artificial techniques, but a very distinctive feeling is created by the way the voice moves freely between the notes played by the instruments. In addition, the clear pronunciation, with every consonant articulated, helps create an effect of austere probity.

D. MUSICAL SCALE

"Jeongdaeeop" uses the musical mode *hwangjong gyemyeonjo*. However, in contrast to the fixed-pitch percussion instruments such as the pyeonjong, pyeon-gyeong, and banghyang, the wind instruments and the vocal part contain a number of places that deviate from hwangjong gyemyeonjo, thus producing considerable disharmony of musical pitch. For example, when the tuned percussion instruments play the tonic hwangjong

(C), the wind instruments and voice may assert resolutely the fourth chungnyeo (F). In this way, there are a number of places in "Jeong-daeeop" where something seems not quite right in the harmony. Yet, in the tension between these conflicting forces, the music seems to gain a more dynamic energy.

E. Rhythmic patterns, beat and tempo

Jongmyo jeryeak is performed at a rather slow tempo throughout. Documents indicate a tempo equivalent to a metronome mark of 50 crotchet (quarter-note) beats per minute for the opening pieces of "Botaepyeong" and "Jeongdaeeop," while "Jeonpye huimun" gets as slow as M.M.=15. In the case of Western music, Grave (slow and solemnly) is about M.M.=40, *Largo* (slow and broad) is about M.M.=46, and *Lento* (slow and weighty) is about M.M.=52. From this comparison one can get a general sense of the tempo range in *Jongmyo jeryeak*.

The rhythmic patterns of *Jongmyo jeryeak* are very distinctive. The rhythmic patterns repeat in very long cycles, so that the majority of pieces consist of only two or three of these cycles. There are also pieces consisting of only a single cycle, or even one-and-a-half cycles. When analyzing the structure of a musical piece, the rhythmic cycle is often used as a basis. Therefore, the irregular rhythmic cycles of *Jongmyo jeryeak* pose some difficulties. For this reason, those who examine this music by the standards of Western music tend to regard it as music with an irregular rhythmic pattern whose beat structure cannot be clearly identified.

Furthermore, when following the score while listening to the music, one can notice discrepancies between what the eyes see on the page and what the ears hear in the music. In particular, the score is divided into *madi* (phrases) by symbols indicating different numbers of beats, but in performance, the beat is freely extended or shortened so that it cannot be read with accuracy as in Western music scores. For this reason, the indications of beats and phrase divisons are practically meaningless. This may have resulted from changes introduced over time by the performers.

F. COMPARISON WITH THE RITE TO CONFUCIUS

The characteristics of *Jongmyo jeryeak* stand out more clearly in comparison with *Munmyo jeryeak*, which is the epitome of regular music set to regular verse. Today's *Munmyo jeryeak* consists of 15 musical pieces, all of them following a fixed form. The length of each piece is the same, as is the duration of each syllable, and even the melodies progress similarly apart from the changes of key. For this reason, a performance of the 15 pieces of *Munmyo jeryeak* in succession sounds like a performace of 15 variations on a theme. Although it unfolds very simply, such music is regarded as the music of noble justice and peace, showing refined beauty in form and balance.

5) APPRECIATION OF REPRESENTATIVE PIECES FROM THE RITE TO ROYAL ANCESTORS

A. 'HUIMUN' AND 'JEONPYE HUIMUN'

'Jeonpye huimun' is a variation of 'Huimun' played in the Yeongsin procedure. Although they use the same melody, when performing for the Jeonpye procedure the variation is produced by prolonging the duration of each beat and expanding the melody. Compared to "Huimun," originally performed at a tempo of each beat lasting about 1.6 seconds, one beat of 'Jeonpye huimun' lasts about 3.7 seconds on average. This alone would be enough to make the piece more than twice as long. In addition, the melodies for wind and string instruments are varied greatly in the third and the fourth of the four phrases that comprise the piece. As in the performance of "Sujecheon," a technique called *yeoneum*, whereby a note is elaborated with additional ornaments, produces a very different musical expression from the original piece. Thus, from the two-minute original, 'Jeonpye huimun' is extended to a duration of about nine minutes, and because of this, it feels like a completely different piece. "Jeonpye huimun" is considered a masterpiece through which one can appreciate the contrast between stately dynamics and elegant melodic beauty. (CD No.3, No.5)

B. 'SOMU' FROM 'JEONGDAEEOP'

Another characteristic piece is "Somu" from "Jeongdaeeop." On the whole, "Jeongdaeeop" has many melodies that unfold powerfully in the high register, with clashes of a major second between hwangjong (C) and *muyeok* (B-flat) produced by the tuned percussion instruments on the one hand and the wind instruments on the other. In "Somu," when the bells and stone chimes play hwangjong, the wind instruments and voice that perform the melody lower this note to muyeok, creating a feeling of tension through the exquisite disharmony. In addition, the melody of "Somu" is played by the taepyeongso (shawm) instead of the dangpiri (oboe). The delightful sound of the taepyeongso clearly reveals that "Jeongdaeeop" is a piece praising military achievement. The sound of the taepyeongso is also heard at the end of the syllable *"mu"* that concludes the lyrics. Elsewhere in *Jongmyo jeryeak*, wind instruments such as dangpiri and daegeum produce a decorative effect between the notes according to the fixed principle called *ganeum*, but the absence of this phenomenon is another characteristic of "Somu." Similar musical characteristics can also be found in "Bunung" and "Yeonggwan." (CD No.4)

III

HISTORY AND CONTEMPORARY STATUS OF
KOREAN RITUAL MUSIC

1. THE ORIGIN AND TRANSMISSION OF RITUAL MUSIC IN KOREA

1) ACCEPTANCE OF AAK IN THE GORYEO DYNASTY

The spirit and culture of ritual music established in the shared cultural area of Northeast Asia was transmitted to Korea in the distant past, but it was not until the 12th century that the sacrificial rite was performed with musical accompaniment. The aak music played at the sacrificial rite could not be purchased with money, nor could the musical pieces be learned. Early on, the Korean intelligentsia became aware, through their studies of Confucian texts, of the existence of aak that Confucius considered "truly good and truly beautiful." They also experienced stately ceremonies accompanied by aak when visiting the Chinese court on frequent occasions. Chinese aak was the envy of national leaders who dreamed of a cultivated state that was governed by ritual and music. But it was not until the reign of King Yejong of Goryeo that the idea of actually providing aak in Korea was put into practice. In the sixth month of 1116, during the 11th year of King Yejong's reign, a company of envoys returned to Goryeo after a visit to Song Dynasty China with a lavish collection of musical instruments and everything that was required for performing a sacrificial rite. This comprehensive set for sacrificial music included 42 kinds of musical instruments and 572 props, costumes for an entire aak performing group, musical scores for musicians, and books that recorded musical playing techniques. How did such a magnificent set of articles for ritual music happen to come to Goryeo?

It is especially intriguing that the set was not purchased by Goryeo with money, but was sent as a gift from Emperor Hui Tsung of Song to Goryeo's King Yejong. What was happening between Goryeo and Song at the time? Let's take a look at the background to the reception of this extravagant gift.

Around this time, Song did not just send musical gifts, nor did Goryeo simply receive gifts from Song. One scholar of Asian studies, who investigated the records of the gifts exchanged between the two countries around the 12th century, found that these countries exchanged all the most valued products, such as paper, ginseng, silk, books, ceramics, and medicines. In the course of this diverse exchange of gifts, some Goryeo envoys to Song received a musical gift from the Emperor Hui Tsung: an instrument set called Daeseongak that was used for playing at a banquet. In 1114, having received a generous gift unexpectedly, Goryeo sent envoys to Song with gifts of their own and a letter of thanks. However, after receiving musical instruments from China, King Yejong of Goryeo realized that a new musical project had been accomplished recently in China, and thought this might be a good time to request a gift of music for court ritual performance rather than banquets. Through the envoys, Yejong sent a letter to Emperor Hui Tsung saying, "The gift of Daeseongak sent last time was received with thanks. However, what Goryeo has long wished for was aak for performing at the state sacrificial rites. If possible, by receiving this aak, we hope to establish a tradition of ritual and music. Please help us so that aak can be performed in Goryeo." Along with the letter, Yejong sent some musicians to accompany the envoys so that they could learn aak if permitted by the Chinese Emperor.

King Yejong's hopes were not disappointed. Emperor Hui Tsung not only taught aak to the musicians from Goryeo but also sent them home with a great number of musical instruments and ceremonial objects. The kinds and numbers of items in this court music were recorded in the *Goryeosa* (History of the Goryeo Dynasty) as follows:

Catalogue of Court Musical Instruments and Ceremonial Objects from Song Dynasty China

Terrace ensemble musical instruments:

Pyeonjong:	16 jeongseong, 12 jungseong
Pyeon-gyeong:	16 jeongseong, 12 jungseong
Geum:	2 each of 1-string, 3-string, 5-string, 7-string, 9-string
Seul:	2
Ji:	2 jungseong, 2 jeongseong
Jeok:	2 jungseong, 2 jeongseong
So:	2 jungseong, 2 jeongseong
Sosaeng:	2 jungseong, 2 jeongseong
Hwasaeng:	2 jungseong, 2 jeongseong
Hun:	2 jungseong, 2 jeongseong
Bakbu:	2
Chuk:	1
Eo:	1

Total: 42 items of 13 kinds

Courtyard ensemble musical instruments:

Pyeonjong:	16 jeongseong (9 sets), 12 jungseong (9 sets)
Pyeon-gyeong:	16 jeongseong (9 sets), 12 jungseong (9 sets)
Geum:	1-string (5), 3-string (13), 5-string (13), 7-string (16), 9-string (16)
Seul:	42
Ji:	24 jungseong, 24 jeongseong
Jeok:	24 jungseong, 24 jeongseong
So:	22 jungseong, 22 jeongseong
Sosaeng:	21 jungseong, 21 jeongseong
Wusaeng:	15 jungseong, 15 jeongseong
Hun:	14 jungseong, 14 jeongseong

Jin-go:	1
Ipgo:	2
Bi-go:	1
Eunggo:	1
Chuk:	1
Eo:	1
Hwibeon:	1

Total: 371 items of 17 kinds

Ceremonial objects for civil dance:

Yak:	36
Jeok:	36
Dok:	2
Hwibeon:	2
Dogo:	2
Yoryeong:	2
Ssangdutak:	2
Geumsun:	2
Sanggo:	2
Geumjeong:	2
Ago:	2

Ceremonial objects for military dance:

Gan:	36
Gwa:	36

Total: 162 items of 13 kinds

Costumes:

- Clothing (gown and hat) for musicians and dancing costumes for ceremonial dancers: one pair each
- Musaekjang: 1 jasu-maraek, 1 jasisuranpo
- One set of clothes for the leader of military dancers: 1 mubyeon-gwan, 1 bisu-maraek, 1 bisisuransam, 1 geumbigu, 1 baekgyonmal-dae, 1 donghyeokdae, 1 opiri
- One set of clothes each for the holders of jeong and dok in the civil and military dances: 1 pyeongmyeon-gwan, 1 josisuransam, 1 donghyeokdae, 1 opiri, 4 heukchilpyogan, etc.

This adoption of aak by Goryeo was an unprecedented event in history. For this reason, various scholars have presented their interpretations concerning the background of the unparalleled musical gift from Song to Goryeo. One theory is that the gift was politically motivated, an attempt by Song to secure military aid from Goryeo in the delicate international political situation of the time. Another interpretation is that it was a positive act of sharing culture by the leaders of two countries whose common concerns were to promote the civilizing effect of ceremony and music. Still another view regards it as an outcome of both Goryeo's intention of trying to establish the Confucian musical system through the acceptance of Chinese traditional aak, and of Goryeo's practical efforts to learn aak by sending musicians along with the diplomatic envoys.

This unprecedented gift of Confucian ceremonial music in the 12th century established a new branch called aak in the history of Korean music that continues to exist to this day.

2) Development and Continuation of Aak

The court ritual music transmitted to Goryeo through this process was called Daeseong aak. Traditionally, it was the custom in China to give a new name to any newly established state music. Daeseong aak is the name referring to the court ritual music established by Emperor Hui Tsung of the Song Dynasty in China. Once aak had been accepted as a national ceremonial music of Goryeo, it began to be performed in the royal household at various sacrificial rites: at Taemyo offered to the ancestors, Won-gu to heaven, Sajik to the gods of earth and grain, and Munseonwangmyo to Confucius. For this, song texts were composed in accordance with the forms of each ceremony, rehearsed with the accompaniment of ceremonial dance, and finally performed with aak at the sacrificial rites, thus establishing a new musical vein in the history of Korean music.

Although the history of Korean aak began successfully with the admiration of the king and ministers, the music went through numerous changes in the following generations. This was because new supplies to sustain the performance tradition of aak were no longer provided from outside, and no foundation had been laid in instrument-making skills or the study of ceremony. Moreover, as conditions in Korea became harder due to military revolts and the Mongol invasion, the transmission of aak accompanying state ceremonies also became endangered. With the country in crisis, musicians gave up their occupation and the instruments and props used in aak performance were in danger of being either lost or seriously damaged.

Nevertheless, the aak tradition continued somehow until the end of the Goryeo Dynasty without becoming extinct. Why did this happen? Generally speaking, the performance tradition of aak survived as long as Confucian politics continued, because aak was cherished not as an object

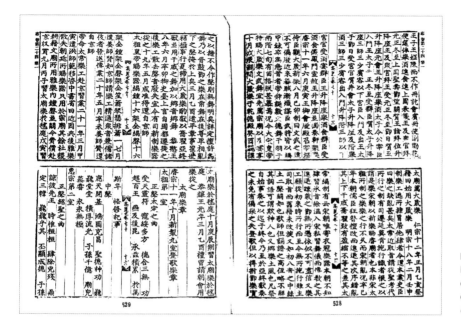

Figure 38
Record of the introduction
of *aak* in "Akji," the chapter
on music from the *History
of the Goryeo Dynasty*.

of musical appreciation but as a kind of symbol that revealed the political stability and wellbeing of a country. The belief that political success was measured through the harmony of ritual and music became the driving force for re-establishing aak immediately after a military crisis or the founding of a new dynasty.

For instance, sacrificial rites were performed with aak when Goryeo moved the capital to Ganghwa Island during the Mongol invasion. Furthermore, King Gongmin (r. 1351-1374), in the process of recovering from a turbulent period and bringing the country to a newfound prosperity, endeavored to establish aak by creating a separate Aakseo in charge of court ritual music. This might reflect the belief that the existence and performance of aak in itself could maintain the symbolic meaning even when the musical instruments and ceremonial objects were in short supply.

Although aak of the Goryeo period went through serious disorder and difficulties in the transmission process, its original function was never completely lost. Instead, the tradition of aak was transmitted to the

Joseon Dynasty through a process called "*hyangakgyoju*," whereby Korean indigenous musical instruments were gradually incorporated into aak performance.

2. MODIFICATION AND RE-CREATION OF RITUAL MUSIC DURING THE JOSEON DYNASTY

On the establishment of the Joseon Dynasty, the task of institutionalizing ritual and composing music was debated as a matter of great importance, and steps were taken to establish a ritual system and provide it with appropriate music. In the fifth year of King Taejong's reign (1404), a petition was made to Ming Dynasty China mentioning the shortage of aak instruments and proposing the purchase of instruments such as pyeonjong and pyeon-gyeong. In response, Ming emphasised that "aak instruments are not the kind of objects that can be purchased privately" and, instead, sent a gift of aak instruments comprising one set of pyeonjong and pyeon-gyeong, four geum, two seul, two saeng and four so. These instruments, although generously donated by Ming, were by no means sufficient to establish the court ritual music of Joseon.

Likewise, the faithful transmission of the music was a difficult task despite continuing efforts to transmit and perform the rites and music in harmony. Not being self-sufficient in the production of aak instruments but depending entirely on China, the harmonization of ritual and music through the recovery of aak was a difficult problem to solve. Such was the situation that the issue of ritual and music emerged as an important matter of national policy during King Sejong's reign (1418-1450).

While Sejong was on the throne, a variety of aak projects were carried out with the aim of improving the imperfect situation of ritual music by

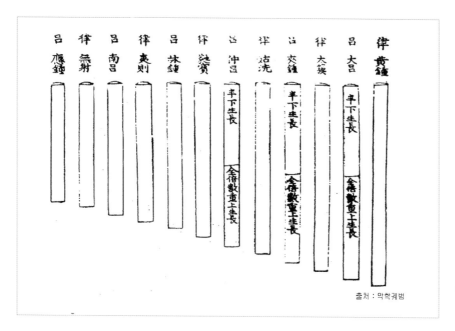

律呂 應鐘 無射 南呂 夷則 林鐘 蕤賓 仲呂 姑洗 夾鐘 太簇 大呂 黃鐘

出처 : 악학궤범

Figure 39
An illustration of 12 musical pitch pipes from *Akhak gwebeom* (1493).

appointing specialists who were knowledgeable in ritual music, studying the original literature, and manufacturing musical instruments. According to the *Annals of King Sejong*, the musical projects of King Sejong's reign began on a very small scale. In the sixth year of King Sejong's reign, Pak Yeon (1378-1458), an official in charge of musical affairs at the Document Archive of the Jangagwon (Board of Music), presented an appeal that caused a stir. He stated: "It is a matter of concern that precious books on ritual music are in danger of being lost due either to a lack of spare copies or to unsuitable conditions for preservation. It is therefore necessary to publish additional copies of literature related to ritual music, which should be housed in the music institute in order to preserve it soundly." Pak Yeon continued to present similar lengthy essay-like appeals on several occasions. This was because, in the process of examining the sources prior to carrying out this task, he realized that the content of the literature on ritual music of Joseon did not correspond to the Chinese *Book of Rites* and that contemporary ritual music was not in accord with any of the original sources. By mobilizing all the resources at his disposal, Pak Yeon pointed out the problems related to ritual music one by one and presented a proposal for reform. The appeal persuasively presented the reasons reform was necessary in everything from the methods of musical performance in accord with ceremonial procedure to matters concerning the musical instruments used in the ceremonies.

Pak Yeon's appeal created an enormous task for King Sejong, but he accepted it wholeheartedly without any objection. Although efforts had been made to correct the state ritual music before King Sejong's reign since the founding of the Joseon Dynasty, the standard of these previous projects served only to highlight the shortcomings of the musical tradition transmitted from the Goryeo Dynasty. In contrast, King Sejong began to approach the matter on a more fundamental basis. The outcome of the musical projects accomplished during King Sejong's reign can be summarized in three areas related to different aspects of the revision of aak.

1) ESTABLISHMENT OF STANDARD PITCH AND MANUFACTURE OF MUSICAL INSTRUMENTS

The musical projects of King Sejong's reign were stimulated when sonorous stone (*gyeongseok*), the material for making pyeon-gyeong, was discovered in Namyang in 1426. Another stimulus came from the production of *geoseo*, a kind of grain necessary for making pitch pipes.

The production of pyeon-gyeong began with the establishment of the standard pitch. In music, the standard pitch is a set frequency of vibration that is prescribed in order to unify the tuning. This standard pitch differs according to geographical and historical context. In the West, the unification of a standard pitch had become an international topic of debate by the late 19th century. As a result, the standard A=435Hz was adopted at conferences in Paris (1859) and Vienna (1885) and came to be widely used internationally. More recently, the United States adopted a concert pitch of A=440Hz that had been decided at a conference held in 1834 in Stuttgart, Germany. This common standard was adopted in order to avoid any clashes in the use of musical instruments and difficulties in performing together when the standard pitch differs from nation to nation.

In contrast, in the Northeast Asian countries there was never much discussion about the establishment of a standard pitch because it was normal to follow the standard set in the suzerain state of aak, China. The problem was that it was difficult to decide what standard to adopt since pitch standards differed between historical periods, as was found during King Sejong's reign when the hwangjong pitch of old pyeonjong and pyeon-gyeong sets was investigated for the production of pitch pipes. In an attempt to solve this problem, Joseon tried to fix the standard pitch based upon a series of theories recorded in the classic texts on music. Pak Yeon, a key figure in this project, discovered after repeated experiments that there was a considerable difference between the original theory and the actual pitch. Consequently, Pak Yeon intended to establish an accurate standard pitch through a thorough investigation of music theory. But, following King Sejong's judgment that "theory alone is not enough to obtain the thing we want," the hwangjong pitch of a pyeongjong set from China was accepted as the standard. It was a practical decision derived from the realization that, after all, the establishment of a standard pitch was merely a matter of making an agreement. Musical instruments were manufactured on the basis of this agreement about the standard pitch, while King Sejong ordered the production of pitch pipes in accordance with the theories, perfecting the theoretical system as well. King Sejong's decision to adopt an agreement on the standard pitch after elaborate study and thorough experimentation was later described as "a blessing from heaven to help our country organize *jeongak* ["proper" or "upright" music] to be transmitted through all generations." It was also significant for the fact that Joseon did such advanced work in the study of musical pitch, which was the foundation of musicological research.

The construction of aak instruments was carried on actively after the material for making pyeon-gyeong was discovered and the standard pitch was established. First mentioned in the eighth lunar month of 1425, the production of pyeon-gyeong began in Namyang, where there was a quarry of the sonorous stone called gyeongseok. From autumn 1427 to summer 1428, about 130 craftsmen and 17 middle-ranking officials participated in producing pyeon-gyeong, and finally 518 stone chimes (about 33 sets of pyeon-gyeong) were completed for use in the various sacrificial rites.

Pyeonjong bells were manufactured at the foundry (*jujongso*) in Mapo on the banks of the Han River. By about the second lunar month of 1429, a comprehensive investigation was under way into the methods of casting, tuning and shaping that are necessary for the production of the bells. By 1430, pyeonjong were being produced for use in sacrificial rites, morning audiences, and social visits (*hoeryeyeon*). Although the number of pyeonjong is not recorded precisely, it is estimated, based upon the number of pyeon-gyeong, that it was probably about 520 bells. In addition, a range of instruments that fell into the categories of silk (*sa*), bamboo (*juk*), gourd (*po*), earth (*to*), skin (*hyeok*), and wood (*mok*) were also manufactured. In the past, it would have been inconceivable to be able to manufacture in so short a time the large quantity of musical instruments that was needed for the various state rites. The large-scale manufacture of musical instruments including pyeon-gyeong and pyeonjong during King Sejong's time testifies to the accumulation of a store of special knowledge and techniques. This technical expertise and knowledge

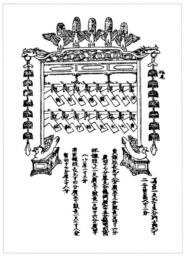

was transmitted to later generations unimpaired. Thus, since King Sejong's time, there has never been a return to the situation where aak could not be performed due to a shortage of musical instruments. This is because a foundation for self-sufficient transmission had been established for state ritual music including aak.

The manufacture of aak instruments also influenced that of Korean indigenous instruments (*hyangakki*) and those of Tang Chinese origin (*dangakki*). In the beginning of the Joseon Dynasty, special institutes called Akki Dogam and Akki Gamjosaek were formed for manufacturing musical instruments, and instruments for the usage of various state ceremonies were freely produced. This is considered a glorious undertaking of technical power that reversed the deficiency of the previous several centuries during which a shortfall in instruments for the state ceremonies was partially met with a supply provided by China upon request.

2) STUDY OF MUSIC THEORY

In 1430 (the 12th year of King Sejong's reign), aak musical pieces were selected for use in the state ceremonies such as sacrificial rites and morn-

Figure 40
An illustration of the manufacture of the stone chime set (pyeon-gyeong) in *Akhak gwebeom*.

Figure 41
A contemporary scene of playing the pyeon-gyeong.

ing audiences. At the same time, the study of music theory also advanced greatly. In particular, concerted efforts were made in the study of *Yullyeo sinseo* that had been recently published in Ming Dynasty China. From 1430, a group of scholars centerd around Jeong In-ji studied this book, and based on their research findings, King Sejong concluded that there was a gap between music theory and practice. As a result, only a selection of the musical pieces in the original repertory for sacrificial rites and morning audiences came in to use. The *Annals of King Sejong* record 144 pieces of sacrificial aak and 312 pieces of morning audience aak, but, in practice, not all the pieces were performed at the sacrificial rites and morning audiences. As for the ritual aak, only "Hwangjonggung" and "Songsin hwangjonggung" were selected from the 144 pieces. In the melody of "Hwangjonggung," all the notes in the upper octave (*cheongseong*) were transposed to the middle octave (*jungseong*), thus resulting in a change of performance style by only employing seven notes. As for the morning audience aak, only two pieces were performed out of the 312: "Yungan-jiak," derived from "Eori," and "Seoanjiak," derived from "Hwanghwangjahwa." These have a song text structure of four characters forming a phrase and four or six phrases forming a verse, and musically they are in the gung mode. "Yungan-jiak" was played for the king's exit and entrance at the morning audiences, while "Seoanjiak" was played for the sovereign's procession and his subjects' respectful salutation.

Here, the aak music for sacrificial rites and morning audiences, which was completed in 1430 and recorded in the scores of the *Annals of King Sejong*, was not a re-creation of the music described in the classic texts on ritual music, but rather a newly established aak reorganized by applying theories from *Yullyeo sinseo*. It was the outcome of meticulous and fundamental research on aak performance, but simplified for practical use without being bound by a complex theoretical system. This helped enormously in preparing a foundation for the practical transmission of aak.

3) SELECTION OF AAK REPERTOIRE

While the project of manufacturing musical instruments was well under way, in 1430 a concerted effort was made to select aak musical pieces for use in state ceremonies such as sacrificial rites and morning audiences. The ritual music transmitted to Sejong's time was based upon 38 song texts of sacrificial rites recorded in *Joseon gugakjang* and tunes used for accompanying the songs that are included in the music score "Sibiyulseong tongnye." However, as Pak Yeon pointed out in his numerous appeals, the system of musical usage for sacrificial music as recorded in *Joseon gugakjang* was incomplete. First of all, although the gung was selected according to the Chou system, the principle of *eumyang hapseong* (union of yin and yang) between the terrace and the courtyard ensembles was not followed. Furthermore, the *Book of Rites* suggested that the terrace and courtyard ensembles should perform alternately according to the ceremonial procedures of the sacrificial rites, but in Sejong's time they performed simultaneously. The Yeongsinak music for welcoming the spirits was performed differently according to the subject of the sacrificial rite: *hyeopjonggung 6 seong* for rites to the gods of heaven (*cheonsin*), *imjonggung 8 seong* for the gods of the earth (*jigi*), and *hwangjonggung 9 seong* for the spirits of the deceased (*in-gwi*); but according to *Joseon gugakjang*, *hwangjonggung 3 seong* should be used for all three rites. Moreover, according to an old decree, the Songsinak music for sending away the spirits should use *yeongsin-gok* 1 *seong* each, but *Joseon gugakjang* states that *hwangjonggung 1 seong* is performed at all sacrificial rites. Because of these inconsistencies, Pak Yeon began by addressing the task of rectifying the system of musical usage of *Joseon gugakjang* in accord with that of the *Book of Rites*.

After correcting the system of musical usage, the selection of aak pieces for use in the sacrificial rites and morning audience went ahead.

The morning audience included the various ceremonies whereby all the governmental officials had an audience with the emperor or king. According to the chapter on rites in *Joseon gyeonggukjeon* (Administrative Code of Joseon), at the beginning of the Joseon Dynasty the "three grand morning audiences" (*samdaejohoe*) were considered of great importance, and comprised Dongji (the winter solstice), *jeongjo*, and birthday celebrations. On these occasions, sovereign and subjects were led to perform the Manggwollye ceremony and the ceremony of receiving the king's royal edict and *samul*. These ceremonies were executed according to the *uiju* (the procedure in the Book of Rite) that was sent from the Chinese government. In addition, there was a small morning audience that was performed on Ipchunil (the onset of spring). Among these ceremonies, aak was provided for use in Samdaejohoe, Manggwollye and Yeongjochik.

In order to do this, a reliable literary source was secured, and selective reforms were applied by examining the content of the original source through a prescribed framework of music theory. For the aak used in sacrificial rites, the sources were *Daeseong akbo* (Ta-sheng Yüeh-p'u) compiled during the Yuan Dynasty and the "Seokjeonak" recorded in *Jijeongjogyeok* (Chih-cheng code, 1345), a kind of code of laws. The aak for use in morning audiences was selected from the "Punga sibibo" repertoire included in Chu Hsi's *Uirye gyeongjeon tonghaesiak*.

In the process of selecting aak pieces, King Sejong as well as other scholars such as Jeong In-ji came to understand the "mystery of production" through their reading of *Yullyeo sinseo* (Lü-lü hsin-shu by Ts'ai Yüan-ting 1135-1198). At a time when the music theory of *jinyang* was widely used, King Sejong was described as a Confucian scholar sent from heaven who had dispelled the public's doubts singlehandedly in his wholehearted adoption of Chae Won-jeong's *Yullyeo sinseo*. However, the word "adoption" here does not imply uncritical acceptance. Toward the end of 1430, having studied *Yullyeo sinseo* for four months, King Sejong came to the conclusion that even *Yullyeo sinseo* could only provide the outward formalities. From the various theories in *Yullyeo sinseo*, only two were selected, as recorded in the *Annals of King Sejong*. These were known as "Aak sibigung chilseongyong isippalseong" and "Sibigung chilseongyong simnyukseong."

As a result, 12 pieces in gung mode were selected for the ritual music from the 16 pieces in *Daeseong akbo*, and these were transposed into 12 keys, making a total of 144 pieces. As for the aak music for the morning audience, 26 pieces in gung mode were selected from the 28 pieces in 6 groups recorded in *Feng-shih* from the *shih ching* (Book of odes), and again these were transposed into 12 keys, making 312 pieces in all.

However, in practice, the entire repertoire of aak pieces for sacrificial rites and morning audiences recorded in the "Aakbo (Notations of Ritual Music)" from the *Annals of King Sejong* was not actually used in performance. As for the ritual aak, only "Hwangjonggung" and "Songsin hwangjonggung" were selected from the 144 pieces. In the melody of "Hwangjonggung," all the notes in the upper octave (*cheongseong*) were transposed to the middle octave (*jungseong*), thus resulting in a change of performance style by only employing seven notes. As for the morning audi-ence aak, only two pieces were performed out of the 312: "Yungan-jiak," derived from "Eori," and "Seoan-jiak," derived from "Hwanghwangjah-wa." These have a song text structure of four characters forming a phrase and four or six phrases forming a verse, and musically they are in the gung mode. "Yungan-jiak" was played for the king's exit and entrance at the morning audiences, while "Seoan-jiak" was played for the sovereign's procession and his subjects' respectful salutation. Here, the aak music for sacrificial rites and morning audiences, which was completed in 1430 and recorded in the scores of the *Annals of King Sejong*, was not a re-creation of the music described in the classic texts on

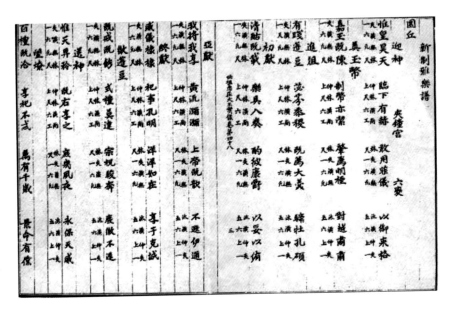

Figure 42
The "Sinje aakbo"
(Notations of Revised Ritual
Music) from the *Annals of
King Sejong.*

ritual music, but rather a newly established aak reorganized by applying theories from the *Yullyeo sinseo*.

The selection procedure described above was based upon the extensive study of original literature and the study of music theory texts such as *Yullyeo sinseo*. These efforts under King Sejong were intended to achieve a complete and well-grounded formulation of aak, which had been incomplete and imperfect prior to the 12th year of Sejong's reign (1430).

The reformed aak at that time was used in several sacrificial rites of the Joseon Dynasty, but later excluded from the performance because, from the 10th year of King Sejo's reign (1464), the Rite to Royal Ancestors came to use mainly "Botaepyeong" and "Jeongdaeeop." Since the fall of the Joseon Dynasty in 1910 and the consequent abolition of state sacrificial rites other than the Rite to Confucius, the use of aak in ceremonies has been drastically reduced. Today, only the Rite to Confucius continues the old tradition of sacrificial music.

THREE LEADERS OF MUSICAL CULTURE
DURING KING SEJONG'S REIGN

• King Sejong (1397-1450)

King Sejong was born on the 10th day of the 4th lunar month in 1397, the third son in his family. His mother was Queen Won-gyeong Hwanghu Minssi. Her name was Do, and she also had the pseudonym Wonjeong. King Sejong was one of the rare rulers who have been knowledgeable about music. In the *Annals of King Sejong*, there are frequent remarks of King Sejong such as, "I understand music to a degree, but when listening to the ritual music, there are times when I have to laugh," or "I understand music fairly well myself. The *namak* [male music] at the current banquets is often out of tune...." Moreover, the *Annals of King Sejong* also recorded that Sejong had a deep understanding of music and had established entire phrases of *sinak* (new music), and that his ear for music was so highly developed that he could identify delicate tonal differences of pyeon-gyeong that went unnoticed by specialists. Furthermore, Sejong's understanding of music treatises and documentation of ritual music was as good as that of any other scholar who participated in the music project. He also devoted himself to the study of music theory by participating in activities such as reading the Ming Chinese text *Yullyeo sinseo*.

King Sejong personally supervised the production of musical pitch pipes as well as the manufacturing processes of musical instruments, official costumes, and ceremonial objects. Before settling on any plan of action, he would go through a process of careful deliberation, consulting such bodies as the Euirye sangjeongso, Yejo (Ministry of Rites), or other groups of specialists, depending on the matter at hand. It is widely known that he was directly involved in the project to manufacture the pitch pipes that set the standard pitch for aak, and when pyeonjong and pyeon-gyeong were produced he requested a trial performance at the Sajeongjeon and reviewed the accuracy of the music in detail.

In addition, King Sejong showed an almost excessive concern for authenticity in arranging the music and dance for banquets, including the movements used by the dancers and the costumes worn by both dancers and musicians. To satisfy Sejong's interest, Pak Yeon and others frequently showed him drawings of musical instruments, costumes, and ceremonial objects that had been created with reference to various historical documents. However, Sejong continued to command them to produce new samples and to present them to him without fail. The documentation of these handmade samples and illustrations was handed down to later generations and collected in the text *Akhak gwebeom*, thus making it possible to transmit permanently the methods for producing musical instruments and ceremonial objects from King Sejong's time.

Sejong also spearheaded a successful music policy by regularly appointing men of ability and providing liberal financial support. In addition to Pak Yeon, he selected Nam Geup, Jeong Yang and Jang Yeong-sil and invited them to take part in the production of musical instruments, in which they rendered distinguished services. The extent of his financial contribution to the establishment of ritual music is suggested by Yu San-ul, who assumed the leadership of the project to assist King Sejong: "Musical instruments such as *jong* and *gyeong* and ceremonial costumes have been provided without counting the immense expense involved, and all of them have been completely renewed within a few years." In discussing the use of dancers for the banquets in the 25th year of his reign (1443), Sejong urged: "If you my servants persevere, why should we not be able to find suitable people even though there are not many? In spite of a shortage of means, I would certainly be prepared to provide. So, you my servants, discuss the merits of the matter."

The accurate understanding of reality that Sejong showed in the course of developing his music policy is truly remarkable. In establishing ritual music, which is apt to be bound by a sense of duty, Sejong's insight in maintaining a balance between duty and reality was one of the most important factors that enabled him to achieve a successful music policy. While pursuing his musical reforms, King Sejong demonstrated a clear standpoint and discernment as to how far reference should be made to Chinese documents on ritual and music. Although Sejong was concerned that "the discord which exists between the music and dance system and the documentation might become a laughing-stock for later generations," he never let his sense of duty make him ignore the reality. Rather than imitate China uncritically or rely on reconstruction from documentary sources, he aimed to perfect a ceremonial music that was more feasible in reality.

As a result, Sejong directly participated in the creation of sinak (new music) in accordance with his own musical ideology, the musical traditions of the Joseon Dynasty, and the theory of ritual music. He also developed a music notation system called *jeongganbo* to transmit this music to later generations. This changed the entire face of Joseon state ceremonial music while laying a foundation for its transmission through the whole 500 years of the Joseon Dynasty.

• Maeng Sa-seong (1360-1438; pseudonym Gobul)

Maeng Sa-seong was born in Onyang, Chungcheongnam-do Province.

He was very knowledgeable about state ceremonies and music of the early Joseon Dynasty from the reign of King Taejo to that of Sejong, and he helped shape the Joseon music policy.

At present, historical records related to Maeng Sa-seong do not reveal anything about his musical training process or his musical ability, but we know that he served as supervisor at the Gwanseup Dogam (Bureau of Music). At that time, the Bureau of Music was responsible for setting to music sinak song texts such as "Monggeumcheok" and "Suborok" that had been composed since King Taejo's time by Jeong Do-jeon and other meritorious subjects involved in the founding of the Joseon Dynasty. Thus, it would not have been possible for Maeng to hold such a position without possessing expertise in music.

When Pak Yeon, who became known for taking a leading role in the music reform project during King Sejong's reign, was still a newcomer, Maeng Sa-seong held the position of *yeongakhak*, a person in charge of the Akhak section of the state music institute, which was responsible for research on music theory and performance usage. In addition, he was not only involved in practical affairs such as musical instrument production, but also presented viewpoints that were influential in shaping the establishment of early Joseon music.

In Sejong's time, opinion on ritual music was divided between Pak Yeon's idea of wholeheartedly accepting Chinese-style aak that accorded with the original sources, and the opposing ideal of establishing a unique tradition for the Joseon Dynasty. Maeng Sa-seong presented an alternative and sagacious policy of combining Chinese and Korean traditions. Today, his idea would be described as the "Korean-style acceptance of foreign culture." Maeng urged that "since tradition and system are liable to variation, it is necessary to cultivate them by revision and supplement according to need, without being bound by theory or sense of duty." His opinion became an important basis for revising state music during the early Joseon Dynasty.

• Pak Yeon (1378-1458; pseudonym Nan-gye)

Born in Yeongdong, Chungcheongbuk-do Province, Pak Yeon was a music theorist and administrative official who, after being promoted to *akhakbyeoljwa* in 1426, devoted his heart and soul to the establishment of aak during King Sejong's reign. According to Seong Hyeon's record, Pak was fluent in *jeottae* (bamboo flute) playing and was also excellent in playing the geomun-go and bipa. However, the family instructions that Pak composed for the raising of his children state that "it would be better to learn the geum and the seul, for the teaching of *samhyeon* music and *gamu* (song and dance) at home is the root of family ruin." Thus, it is possible to assume that his outstanding instrumental performance skill would not have been exposed on frivolous occasions. Referring to this statement, some scholars have concluded that Pak Yeon valued Chinese music (geum and seul) over Korean (samhyeon and gamu). But rather than equating "samhyeon and gamu" with Korean music and "geum and seul" with Chinese, one could interpret these terms as referring, respectively, to music for entertainment contexts and to the music for string instruments that scholars play to cultivate their sensibilities. Such an interpretation gives a better understanding of the music that Pak intended to encourage.

Pak Yeon passed the civil service examination in 1411 (the 11th year of King Taejong's reign), and after King Sejong's enthronement he was appointed as supervisor at the Gwanseup Dogam and undertook the task of supervising music. From then on, Pak worked on pitch pipes based on his extensive reading of a wide range of musical literature and studies of music theory, and personally carried out studies and experiments in musical instrument making. He devoted all his energies to establishing a system that would enable aak to be performed at sacrificial rites, morning audiences, and banquets. As a result, he stimulated the study of music theory during the early Joseon Dynasty and helped provide a solid basis for transmitting Chinese-style aak, whose tradition survives in the Rite to Confucius today.

3. THE ORIGIN OF KOREAN-STYLE RITUAL MUSIC AND ITS CONTEMPORARY TRANSMISSION

1) THE BIRTH OF JONGMYO JERYEAK

The *Jongmyo jeryeak* performed today was created under King Sejong to praise his ancestors' great achievements in contributing to the foundation and subsequent development of the Joseon Dynasty. Although King Sejong took a deep interest in developing various measures for reforming state ritual music, he also produced new music of Joseon that he wished to propagate widely among the people. Song texts were composed to express even more powerfully the merits and virtues of the past kings who strove for the foundation of the Joseon Dynasty and for national prosperity and the welfare of the people, and these were performed in ceremonies with the accompaniment of musical instruments and dance. By doing so, sovereign and subject who gathered together at ceremonies and banquets were to remember the significance of the founding of the country in their hearts.

Sejong, however, believed that the use of aak alone had its limits, so he presented a number of pieces in which elements derived from Korean indigenous music hyangak and non-ritual Chinese music (dangak) were incorporated. These pieces included "Jeongdaeeop," "Botaepyeong," "Balsang," and "Bongnaeui," which extolled the glorious merits of the king's ancestors and the hardships they experienced in founding the dynasty. These musical pieces were to be used for various state ceremonies. The following record from the *Annals of King Sejong* reveals King Sejong's thoughts:

Now the reason that Yongbieocheon-ga was given was for singing

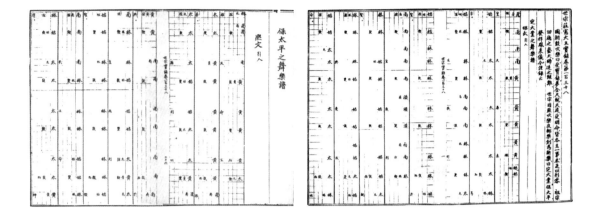

Figure 43
Scores of "Botaepyeong" and "Jeongdaeeop" recorded in the *Annals of King Sejong*.

and reciting the abundant virtues and holy merits of the royal ancestors.... It would not be right if its use were to be restricted to the Rite to Royal Ancestors only. Thus, music such as "Yeomillak," "Chihwapyeong," and "Chipunghyeong" should be permitted to be used commonly at pubic and private banquets. However, a system for their specific use should be in place: for example, "Yeomillak man" should be used for the morning audience and when going out of the palace on days when royal or governmental letters are dispatched; "Yeomillak yeong" should be used on the day of returning to the palace for the morning audience and of visiting to dispatch a letter or money or receive a royal edict. "Hwangjonggung" should be used on all these occasions. "Yeomillak man" should be played when rising to the throne on the day of morning audience at the Gyejodang temple, and "Yeomillak yeong" when returning to the palace. "Goseon-gung" should be used for these occasions.

King Sejong put especially great efforts into composing "Botaepyeong" and "Jeongdaeeop," which expressed, respectively, the civil and the military virtues of the past kings who had laid down a solid foundation for the country through the establishment of a new dynasty, the strengthening of national defence and the correction of national

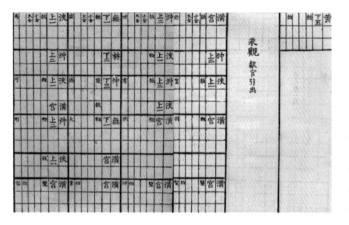

Figure 44
The *Daeak hubo* score a
music of the Rite to Royal
Ancestors (collection of the
National Center for Korean
Traditional Performing
Arts).

order so that the people could live as cultured citizens. "Botaepyeong-jiak," praising the civil merits of laying a firm foundation in cultural politics, and "Jeongdaeeop," praising the military merits of preserving self-defence and national prosperity and the welfare of the people, were large-scale musical compositions comprising a total of 26 pieces of irregular Chinese verse (11 in "Botaepyeong" and 15 in "Jeongdaeeop") with civil and military dances.

In this composition, Sejong made a radical innovation by combining aak with hyangak and dangak on an equal basis. As a result, a new form was created that did not exist in the Joseon Dynasty before. This form included a combined composition of instrumental music, song, and dance; the akjak and akji parts signalling, respectively, the beginning and ending of the terrace ensemble music; the principle of unifying the beginning and ending note; and the instrumentation including pyeon-jong, pyeon-gyeong, chuk, and eo. Moreover, a kind of arrangement method was employed for the completion of "Botaepyeong" and "Jeongdaeeop" whereby the basic musical material was selected from Goryeo songs such as "Cheongsan byeolgok" and "Gasiri" and these were revised to fit new song texts. As a result, unique compositions were created containing familiar tunes which could be appreciated in a new instrumental arrangement and performance style. This innovation could

Figure 45
Front cover of *Sogak wonbo*, an 18th century music score that recorded the music of the Rite to Royal Ancestors (collection of the National Center for Korean Traditional Performing Arts).

Figure 46
Ritual music from the *Sogak wonbo*.

Figure 47
Front cover of the *Jongmyo akki joseongcheong uigwe* that recorded the manufacturing of the instruments used at the Rite to Royal Ancestors (collection of Gyujanggak).

be described as the "crossover" music of the Joseon Dynasty.

This music was first performed at the state banquet rather than the sacrificial rite, where ritual music revised in the Chinese aak style was being performed at that time. However, King Sejong considered this a problem, pointing out that "Our ancestors listened to Korean indigenous music when alive, but after death they listen to Chinese aak. This is contrary to reason." In addition, the new music was created with the intention that the composition praising the great work of the ancestors who contributed to the foundation of the development of the dynasty should be something that was more familiar to the people. Thus, Sejong must have hoped to use this music in the sacrificial rites of the dynasty some day. Sadly, however, Sejong passed away without accomplishing this dream. The wishes of King Sejong were handed down to King Sejo, and finally "Botaepyeong-jiak" and "Jeongdaeeop-jiak" were selected as the music for the Rite to Royal Ancestors in the 10th year of King Sejo's reign (1464).

King Sejo put aside the common assumption that aak must be performed for sacrificial rites, and firmly proclaimed his intention to replace aak with indigenous music (*sogak*) by accepting "Botaepyeong" and "Jeongdaeeop" for performance at the sacrificial rites to the late kings who used to enjoy Korean hyangak when alive. He then revised "Botaepyeong" and "Jeongdaeeop" in a style befitting ritual music and began to have them performed at the sacrificial rites. As a result, a number of changes were introduced to these pieces. The original 11 pieces of "Botaepyeong" and 15 of "Jeongdaeeop" were revised as 11 pieces each; the song texts were either shortened or rearranged to suit the ritual music; and new content was added to make the pieces more like ritual music. For example, the texts now included the pledge, "If the ancestors bless us, it will not be forgotten for a long time"; the wish, "May you secure the prosperity of your descendents and see their success forever"; and the request, "Please bring happy events to the descendents who are dutiful to their parents and protect them that they may enjoy a long life." Furthermore, Chinese-style "Pungan-jiak" music was used for the ritual procedures of Jinchan (presenting food offerings) and Cheolbyeondu (gathering up the ceremonial utensils), while "Heungan-jiak" was used for sending off the spirits. Thus, in the 10th year of King Sejo's reign, the *Jongmyo jeryeak* went through a number of changes including the revision and supplementation of King Sejong's "Botaepyeong" and "Jeongdaeeop-jiak" in favor of a style better suited to ritual music and the addition of music needed for the procedures of the rite. In this way, *Jongmyo jeryeak* entered a new era and was developed into the form that exists today.

2) Contemporary Transmission of Ritual Music

Since the fall of the Joseon Dynasty, the state sacrificial rites of that dynasty have gone through considerable changes. Of the six sacrificial rites involving musical performance, only the Rite to Royal Ancestors and the Rite to Confucius have survived. Currently, both sacrificial rites are preserved and transmitted as Important Intangible Cultural Properties, while the Rite to Royal Ancestors and its music have also been designated by the international UNESCO committee as a Masterpiece of the Oral and Intangible Heritage of Humanity. Nevertheless, the symbolism and meaning that the rites had in the dynastic period have been much weakened. In the face of a sudden influx of Western culture, the value of tradition rapidly declined, and concern for tradition tended to be forgotten as Korea went through the Japanese colonial period and the Korean War. In the process, much intangible heritage was lost, but due to the ties maintained by the Yi Wang-jik Aak-bu and the National Center for Korean Traditional Performing Arts, the music and dance which is the nucleus of the sacrificial rite has fortunately been preserved to this day.

The UNESCO committee had already recognized the Korean Royal Ancestral Shrine (Jongmyo) as worthy of protection for all humanity, appointing it as World Cultural Heritage Site No. 738 in December 1995. Since the selection of the Rite to Royal Ancestors (Important Intangible Cultural Property No. 56) and its music *Jongmyo jeryeak* (Important Intangible Cultural Property No. 1) as a Masterpiece of the Oral and Intangible Heritage of Humanity in May 2001, public interest in the ritual music has increased. With the development of digital content projects to disseminate information about the architecture of the Royal Ancestral Shrine, the Rite to Royal Ancestors, the ritual music, and its value, since 2001 it has been possible to provide systematic specialist information about the Rite to Royal Ancestors. Moreover, in addition to the annually held Rite to Confucius and Rite to Royal Ancestors, the performances of *Jongmyo jeryeak* (2002) and *Munmyo jeryeak* (2003) which were given in order to reconstitute them as stage works were well received as a new stage form of traditional performing arts. Yet the authenticity and accuracy of the sacrificial rite and its music and dance, which were transmitted with great difficulty over the last hundred years ignored by the general public, have recently become a subject of debate. Questions concerning the similarity and differences between the costumes worn at the sacrificial rites today and those of the Joseon Dynasty, and between the content of the ritual music and that of the Joseon Dynasty, continue to be raised. It has also been questioned whether the *kwanghaeng* (routine practice) of instrumental playing, singing, and dancing was done correctly during the days when the transmission of music and dance was so difficult, as it had been in the past. In response, professional institutions such as academic circles and the NCKTPA have held, in addition to musical performances, public lectures on ritual music or organized demonstrations with reconstructed costumes worn by the instrumental players and dancers.

The concern for ritual music described heretofore should help make the transmission of ritual music even more secure, because the diversified study and examination of the ritual music which was once transmitted among a small number of professional musicians as "routine practice" would facilitate the transmission of the tradition of Korean ritual music as a unique cultural heritage that gives true insights into an ancient historical culture of Northeast Asia.

REFERENCES

AUDIO RECORDINGS:

Jongmyo jeryeak (SKC, 1987)

Han-guk eumak seonjip je 29 jip – Jongmyo jeryeak (Gungnip Gugagwon, 2006)

Saenghwal gugak daejeonjip je 9 jip – chumowa giwon-ui eumak (Seoul Eumban, 1994)

VIDEO RECORDINGS:

Jongmyo, jongmyodaeje (VHS) (Gaya Peurodeoksyeon, 1997)

Jongmyo jeryeak (DVD) (Gungnip Gugagwon, 2004)

MUSIC SCORES:

Gugak jeonjip (*jeongganbo*) *18 jip – Jongmyo jeryeak* (Gungnip Gugagwon, 2006)

PHOTOGRAPHIC COLLECTIONS:

Jongmyo (Photographs: Bae Byeongwu; Text: Yi Sanghae and Song Hyejin), Samsung Munhwa Jaedan, 1998.

A P P E N D I X   I

SONG TEXTS OF RITUAL MUSIC:

THE ORIGINALS AND TRANSLATIONS OF THE FULL TEXTS

Song Texts of the Rite to Confucius

1. Yeongsin – "Eungan-jiak"

"Eungan-jiak" in the Yeongsin procedure welcomes the sage Confucius as the greatest teacher venerated by the people of the whole world.

How great, O sage, your ethics and virtuous conduct so high!
Embodying the teaching of the royal way, you are recognized as the head of the whole human family.
We offer you this sacrificial rite with purity and sincere devotion,
And as you descend among us, your appearance itself is holy.

2. Jeonpye – "Myeongan-jiak"

"Myeonganjiak" in the Jeonpye procedure asks Confucius to accept the ceremonial offerings and foods that have been prepared with humble courtesy.

Ever since people first appeared in the world, who can match the holy virtue of Confucius?
Only the spirit of King Munseon surpassed the sages of former times.
Gifts and sacrificial offerings are prepared thoroughly and the ceremony is performed with dignity;

Even if the sacrificial offering lacks something and is not fragrant, please hear our prayer!

3. CHOHEON – "SEONGAN-JIAK"

Originally, the Choheon procedure had song texts devoted to four sages, of whom Confucius was one, but today it only uses "Seonganjiak" in honor of Confucius. The content asks the sage to take pleasure in the sacrificial rite that pays tribute to his heaven-sent virtue.

> Great, O great, is the virtue bestowed from heaven.
> Worshipping with musical accompaniment, the rite will not cease.
> The wine that fills the glass is fragrant, and the meat offerings are ample.
> Please come and partake of these foods offered to a god.

4. AHEON AND JONGHEON – "SEONGAN-JIAK"

The Aheon and Jongheon procedures both use the same song. The content states that the sacrificial rite is concluded by offering three glasses of wine to the great teacher of Confucianism who showed the people how to live.

> You are a teacher above all kings and a way for all people to live.
> The more we look upon you, the more your virtue overflows; please, god, stay with us.
> The golden glass filled up with wine and offered to you is clear and fragrant.
> After offering three glasses of wine we end the rite with a joyful heart.

5. CHEOLBYEONDU – "OAN-JIAK"

"Oanjiak" in the Cheolbyeondu procedure accompanies the procedure of gathering up the ceremonial utensils. It sings that as the sacrificial rite has been presented with pure sacrificial offerings, the people are in harmony and the gods are pleased.

Huijun and *sangjun* are placed in front and *byeon* and *du* are arranged left and right.

Since a sacrificial rite is being offered, they are fragrant and clean.

As the ceremony and music are properly arranged, the people are in harmony and the gods are pleased.

Performing a sacrificial rite brings blessings, and there is no violation against the codes of the ceremony.

6. Songsin – "Eungan-jiak"

"Eungan-jiak" in the Songsin procedure is the song for sending off the gods after completing the whole sacrificial rite. It contains a prayer to the departing god, after gladly receiving the sacrificial rite offered with such sincerity, to bestow abundant blessings on all.

To the noble palace of learning where the sages are in attendance, people come from all directions to meet the teachers.

The sight of a sacrificial rite presented with true devotion is benign.

As you go back suddenly on a wind-borne carriage after enjoying the food offerings at the sacrificial table,

The sacrificial rite comes to an end. Please grant us all boundless blessings.

Song Texts of the Rite to Royal Ancestors

1. Yeongsin – "Huimun"

With virtue cultivated from generation to generation, you lead us, your descendents.

Ah, ah! We can readily imagine that sight and sound.

Solemnly and in accordance with etiquette, the sacrificial rite is offered with care.

Please make us comfortable and grant our wishes.

2. Jeonpye – "Huimun"

Although these ceremonial offerings are things of no value, we hope you will come to like them.

We proffer this basket to present our gifts.

If the ancestors were to enjoy this with pleasure,

This mind that respectfully offered the ceremony would be at peace.

3. Jinchan – "Pungan-jiak"

Food made with true devotion

We offer in the sacrificial utensils.

After serving food on the sacrificial utensils,

Music is played according to the procedure,

And incense is burnt in the dutiful performance of the rite.

Please, god, help us.

4. CHOHEON – "BOTAEPYEONG-JIAK"

1) "Huimun"

That the holy ancestors opened up a bright path

And reigned with a bright and beautiful culture, is clearly apparent.

To praise this noble undertaking,

We can only compose and sing this song.

2) "Gimyeong"

Ah, ah! Holy Mokjo

Crossed the sea and moved to the land of Gyeongheung,

As the number of converts increased day by day,

In this place he consolidated the foundation of heaven's will.

3) "Gwiin"

The great Emperor,

Seeking a place for the people to live,

Went around every corner of the country,

Spreading bright virtue.

Because you said that we cannot lose good people,

All kinds of people followed like a shadow.

Although people crowded together like in a market place,

You did not think of them as following you personally.

You did not think of it personally,

But said they were only showing devotion to good.

Because you considered it as only showing devotion to good,

You were able to secure an even broader foundation.

4) "Hyeongga"

Ah! The great and holy Ikjo

Obeyed the king of Goryeo,

And the great Dojo also followed his will,

Winning the deep trust of the king of Goryeo.

Their efforts were crowned with beautiful success,

And by heaven's command they came to govern the country.

5) "Jimnyeong"

Ssangseong was such a distant place

That people used to call it the land of heaven.

Because the government officials controlling this place did not fulfil their duties,

It had been a place where the people could not enjoy even one day's peace.

However, Hwanjo governed it harmoniously and peacefully,

So that the people who had wandered away came back at last.

With heaven's love, you received a command

And established great blessings.

6) "Yunghwa"

Ah, ah! Great and holy founding king Taejo,

Your virtue is great.

With kindness you made people comfortable, with justice you made them obedient,

Your holy teaching was abundant and ample.

From the barbarians who came from a distant island

To the barbarians in the mountains,

You embraced them all with a kind heart,

So that there was no one who did not follow you.

Some came by boat, some came riding on a ladder,

Lining up to follow the founding king Taejo.

Ah! The shining spirit of King Taejo

Made nearby places peaceful and distant places solemn.

7) "Hyeonmi"

Ah! Great and holy King Taejong

Stabilized the country in a great crisis and preserved the sovereignty peacefully.

Although songs praised King Taejong's merits and public confidence in him was high,

He insisted on yielding the throne, showing outstanding virtue.

8) "Yonggwangjeongmyeong"

As the Emperor of China was reported to be angry,

The people of Goryeo trembled in terror and were very much afraid.

King Taejong went to see the Emperor

And showed his loyalty,

And the Emperor considered him worthy,

So glorious was the king's virtue.

His kind and beautiful queen

Was the honorable consort of the great King Taejong.

When King Taejong stabilized the country in a great crisis,

She helped him with clear wisdom.

Ah, ah! As you are so righteous and pure,

There is no limit to the blessings you shower on us.

9) "Junggwang"

Ah, ah! Great ancestors,

Your noble virtue shines out again and again!

By revealing mistakes to the Chinese Emperor,

You set the heads of our families straight.

By observing righteousness, you drove out the barbarians

And secured our borders.

By receiving blessings, you opened up the way ahead for your descendants

Which will shine and flourish eternally.

10) "Daeyu"

Yeoljongjo shone out again and again,

Governing all places peacefully with civil virtue.

As the law and system are already firmly established,

How brilliant is the great kingship.

11) "Yeokseong"

What the ancestors sought through the generations while cultivating virtue,

Is the great task that we are following.

Their light revealed a peaceful reign,

In which ceremony and music flourished all around.

With the *yak* held in the left hand and the *jeok* in the right,

The music is played nine times,

Revealing the virtue and fervor of the ancestors

So that all kinds of beauty and good deeds spread far and wide.

5. Aheon, Jongheon – "Jeongdaeeop-jiak"

1) "Somu"

To help and protect our glorious armies,

Heaven has let fortune in war shine through the generations,

Promoting distinguished services beyond compare,

And for this we sing and dance in praise.

2) "Dokgyeong"

Our great and holy Mokjo

Raised morale among the troops in the north.

By promoting a happy outcome in this way,

He paved the way for the foundation of our kingship.

3) "Takjeong"

When gangs of aggressive barbarians

Occupied Ssangseong castle,

Our great Hwanjo

Mowed them down completely.

By eradicating these gangs of crafty bandits,

He secured our borders.

4) "Seonwi"

Ah, ah! As Goryeo was not being ruled properly,

Foreign invaders attacked whenever possible.

Island barbarians were plundering at random,

Robbers of Nahachu looked around at will with glaring eyes,

Red Turban Bandits ran amok and swaggered,

Remnants of the Wen Kingdom got angry,

Treacherous Buddhist monks were rampant,

And the ringleaders of the barbarians rampaged at will.

Our great Taejo

Mustered holy military might,

Displaying the dignity of Heaven.

How glorious and majestic he was!

5) "Sinjeong"

When he became enraged with the enemy,

He punished them like felling a tiger with an axe.

In his famous bravery,

He seemed to fly through the air.

The whole sky trembled.

It was righteous and wonderful.

Like a tiger trying to fight an axe,

The enemy fell down by itself at once,

Destroyed like split bamboo.

Who could dare oppose us?

To achieve such complete stabilization by military merit

Is the realm of gods, not people.

6) "Bunung"

We are strong and brave,

Like the thunder and lightening.

No matter how firm they stand, can we not break them down?

No matter how great the danger, can we not restore tranquility?

When we take prisoners of war in row after row,

They are struck dumb as the ears of those who do not obey are cut off and offered up.

The moment we brandish the divine shield and sword,

The air of treachery has vanished at once.

We need not brook contempt or annoyance:

Be prosperous, our country!

7) "Suneung"

When King Sinu of Goryeo declined a royal petition

And dared to start a war,

King Taejo came to a clear decision

And withdrew our troops to Songdo Island,

And both heaven and the people helped him.

8) "Chongsu"

Hereupon, a rightful flag was turned back,

And as he was obedient to heaven's will, heaven helped him greatly.

Heaven trembled, thinking this noble,

And the people rejoiced all together.

While expecting love and peace from the beloved,

They welcomed him with food in a jar.

Now that filth and sin were washed away,

Our country would be clear forever like the Eastern Sea.

9) "Jeongse"

When Jeong Mongju, that lonely loyal statesman of the Goryeo Dynasty,

Instigated an opportunity for calamity,

Our ancestor

Discovered the secret plot

And rooted it out with his mysterious wisdom,

Thus making the world peaceful.

10) "Hyeokjeong"

When the island barbarians rashly

Harassed our frontier,

He showed his anger

And mustered our military troops.

Ten thousand boats under full sail

Crossed the sea as if flying,

Overturned the den,

And attacked the lair,

As though plucking feathers from a wild goose,

And burning them in blazing flames.

Waves as huge as a whale calmed down again,

Our country became peaceful forever and ever.

11) "Yeonggwan"

Ah, ah! Our ancestors

Had military virtue through the generations.

Such flourishing virtues and great achievements

How can we possibly describe?

There is order in our dance;

The exit and ending are in accordance with the rules,

And a dignified and leisurely melody

Is drawn out at length to mark the end.

6. Cheolbyeondu – "Eungan-jiak"

We serve the offerings in the ceremonial utensils

Until they overflow the wooden and bamboo utensils.

As the sacrificial offerings presented are fragrant,

We know that the ancestral spirits have been here.

Completing the sacrificial rite that we have offered,

We announce the clearing of the sacrificial table.

7. Songsin – "Heungan-jiak"

As the sacrificial rite was held according to the rules,

Were you spirits feeling comfortable and delighted?

Before going any further on your way,

Turn your head to look at us once more.

Riding on clouds that look like a rainbow banner,

You depart into the distance.

A P P E N D I X I I

SEARCHING FOR SOUND HARMONY FROM NATURAL RESOURCES:
MUSICAL INSTRUMENTS FOR RITUAL MUSIC

About 2,000 B.C., people in Northeast Asia, including Korea, discovered eight sounding materials among the objects that existed in nature, and began to have a systematic understanding about making and playing musical instruments using these materials. That is, they regarded the sounds of *pareum* (the "eight sounds" produced by metal, stone, silk, bamboo, gourd, earth, skin, and wood) as musical sounds, and became interested in the question of what material the instruments were made of. This notion greatly influenced the establishment of a distinctive musical culture that differed from that of the old Western society in which musical instruments were categorized by the method of playing as wind instruments, percussion instruments, and string instruments. The belief that the materials originated from nature, and therefore that the balanced matching of these materials would create the most musical effect, helped lay the foundation for a unique musical culture.

In Korea, ever since *aak* (court ritual music) began to be performed at the state sacrificial rites in the 12th century, the tradition of the Rite to Confucius, in which the musical arrangement is based upon instruments representing the "eight sounds," has been preserved authentically, and the "eight sounds" system is also considered important in the general classification of musical instruments. That is, although the "eight sounds" classification system was originally applied to aak imported from China, in Korea the system and the symbolism of musical instruments were importantly discussed in the musical treatise *Akhak gwe-beom* (1493), and from the 18th century, when the music of sacrificial rites began to use instruments from *hyangak* (music of Korean origin) and *dangak* (music of Chinese origin) as well as aak, these too began to be classified according to the "eight sounds" system. In the following section, musical instruments used in *Munmyo jeryeak* (music for the Rite to Confucius) and *Jongmyo jeryeak* (music for the Rite to Royal Ancestors) are examined according to this system.

METAL SOUND

According to the pareum classification system that categorizes the main materials of musical instruments into eight kinds, the instruments that belong to the "metal sound" category include *pyeonjong* (bronze bell set), *teukjong* (single bronze bell), *banghyang* (iron slab set), *jing* (large gong) and *kkwaenggwari* (small gong). Ever since people of the Bronze Age began to cast metal into bells, xylophone-like slabs, and circular percussion instruments, bell sets with distinctive tonal systems have been made and used as an important part of state sacrificial rites and other ceremonies in Northeast Asia. Among instruments of the "eight materials," the pyeonjong was considered an indispensable musical instrument in the tradition of sacrificial rites, and exceptional attention was paid to its manufacture, storage, and performance. Bells had to be made according to fixed requirements, and the person responsible was severely punished if the instrument was damaged due to careless storage. In addition, there was a regulation stating that the bells had to be given special protection during war. Generally, the resonating metallic sounds that are unique to metal instruments were understood as a symbol of dignity and grandeur. They also symbolized the season of the vernal equinox in late autumn, and the compass direction west.

The metal instrument pyeonjong is paired with the *pyeon-gyeong* (stone

Pyeonjong   Jing

chime set) made of trimmed jade slabs, and is played with the multiple
bells suspended on a frame. There was once an astonishing discovery of
a set comprising 64 suspended bells found among ancient Chinese
relics. The 64 bells were tuned according to size, from one as small as a
fist to one as tall as a child, and ranged in several rows. Several other
forms of bell sets were also cast in China.

Korea, on the other hand, has continued to use one form of pyeonjong
since the acceptance of aak from China in the 12th century. The rows of
bells are all of the same size, but their pitch is varied by differences in
thickness. In shape, unlike the Chinese bells which are straight from top
to bottom, the Korean bells are characterized by a curved line, an oval
base, and a protruding circular boss on the surface. This device helps
produce a beautiful sound while preventing it from lingering too long.

The bells are hung in two rows on a specially designed frame. Eight bells
covering the chromatic scale from *hwangjong* (C) to *imjong* (G) are
arranged from right to left on the lower rank, while eight more bells
extending from *ichik* (A-flat) to *cheonghyeopjong* (E-flat) are arranged
from left to right on the upper rank. Metal hangers are attached to the
frame for hanging the bells with ease. To play the pyeonjong, the bells

are struck with a cow's horn mallet wedged into a wooden handle.

The structure and manufacturing techniques of the Korean pyeonjong were studied extensively in the 15th century under King Sejong's policy of musical reconstruction. Specific techniques developed during this period for casting alloys and tuning the bells were recorded in detail and have been passed down to this day. The pyeonjong has the same number of bells as the pyeon-gyeong has stone slabs so that the two will be in harmony when placed symmetrically to each other. On the other hand, the teukjong (single bronze bell), which is always played together with the pyeonjong in the music for the sacrificial rites, was tuned to the hwangjong note of the pyeonjong and played to signal the start of the music. In contrast to the pyeonjong and teukjong used in aak, the banghyang (iron slab set), which is a kind of tuned metallic percussion instrument, was employed in the splendid banquet music of the palace. The iron slabs were arranged on a wooden frame like that of a xylophone. In addition, the metallic percussion instruments jing and kkwaeng-gwari, symbolic of valiant military prestige, are played in the performance of "Jeongdaeeop" at the Rite to Royal Ancestors to praise the military achievements of the ancestors.

STONE SOUND

The material for the stone section is a special kind of jade that resonates clearly when struck. Because this jade is used for making chimes, it is called *gyeongseok* (chime stone). As this chime stone was only found within a small area, the instruments in this category were regarded as producing a precious and special sound. The sound of stone chimes was considered light, warm and soft compared with that of the pyeonjong and teukjong that were paired with the chimes. Among the 24 seasonal divisions of the year, the stone chimes symbolized Ipdong, the onset of winter. The clear and distinctive sound of each note on the chimes expressed def-

Pyeon-gyeong

initeness in reasoning and judgment, and was also regarded as a sound that reminded government officers to do their duty even at the risk of their life in extreme situations.

There are two instruments in the stone category: the pyeon-gyeong with 16 slabs suspended on a frame and the *teukgyeong* with a single slab, also hung from a frame. The pyeon-gyeong and teukgyeong sounds give an impression of purity and unique elegance that springs from the natural stones. The low notes of the pyeon-gyeong have lingering after-tones that are soft and rich in volume, while the chimes of the high register produce shorter and clearer after-tones. The teukgyeong is tuned to hwangjong (C), the main tonic note of aak, and plays in the musical phrase that signals the ending of a piece in the sacrificial rites.

Until the early 15th century, Korea had mainly imported these instruments from China. However, research and experiment on manufacturing musical instruments were extensively carried out as chime stone producing sites were identified for the first time in Korea during King Sejong's reign. As a result, a very traditional and superior manufacturing technique for chime stones was secured, making Korea independent in the maintenance of the tradition.

Silk Sound

The instruments included in this category of the "eight sounds" classification system are the string instruments such as the *geum* and *seul* played in aak, the *geomun-go* and *gayageum* that are the main stringed instruments of Korea, and the bowed chordophones *haegeum* and *ajaeng*.

The strings of these instruments are made of fine silk threads extracted from a cocoon and twisted together in several layers. The sound of these silk strings is warm and soft compared with that of metallic wire, nylon, or gut strings. The zithers geum, seul, gayageum, and geomun-go have strings of varying thickness attached to a long rectangular wooden resonance box. The delicate sound of silk thread, enhanced by the vibration of the paulownia wood resonance box, has a subtle, elegant and noble quality. In terms of seasons, it symbolizes the summer solstice.

String instruments have traditionally been closely associated with the image of an intellectual and are symbols of a refined cultural life. An ancient music book advises that "when a man's state of mind is distracted, listening to sad music will make him truthful and honest; when in a sorrowful and wretched state of mind, it will bring a strong determination to resolve the matter and curb one's trivial desires. As the sound of stringed instruments can trigger such a state of mind, all men of culture should learn a stringed instrument and play it in their moments of leisure."

Furthermore, it is even suggested in the *Analects of Confucius* that the word "*geum*" (stringed instrument) conveys the meaning of its homophone "*geum*" (keeping away) and that stringed instruments therefore have the effect of keeping a distracted mind away. Thus, gentlemen are advised never to be apart from their instruments except when absolutely necessary. Particularly, both Chinese *qin* and Korean geomun-go were synonymous with the intellectual music that represented the culture of the literati. At the same time, they were transmitted as the instruments of the free hermit who cut himself off from worldly desire and lived in retirement with nature.

Geum AND *Seul*

The seven-stringed zither geum (Chinese qin), an important string instrument of Northeast Asia, is also called the *hwigeum* signifying the fact that its fingerboard is inlayed with mother-of-pearl. The seul, which always plays with the geum in ritual music, is a large instrument with 25 strings. The top of its large and capacious resonance box is decorated with designs of clouds and cranes that are flying away, elaborately portrayed in eye-catching colors such as orange, white, and black on a light green ground. Today, these instruments are played in the Rite to Confucius only.

Geum

Seul

Geomun-go AND *Gayageum*

Since its creation in the Kingdom of Goguryeo (?-668), the geomun-go has been handed down as the instrument producing the sound that is the most characteristic of Korea. On a long rectangular resonance box, 16 frets of varying heights are fixed, and 6 strings are stretched over the

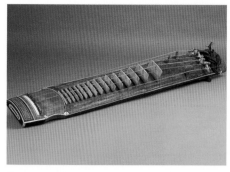
Geomun-go

Gayageum

frets. When playing, the left hand is placed on the string before each note is sounded, and the right hand strikes the stings with a bamboo stick called *suldae* to produce the sound. The thick strings of the geomun-go produce a dark and heavy sound, giving an impression of solemnity.

The gayageum is a 12-string instrument originating in the ancient kingdom of Gaya and transmitted through the Silla Kingdom. Movable bridges known as *anjok* (literally "goose feet") are arranged on the soundboard like wild geese flying away, and the strings are strung over the bridges. The sounds are produced by plucking or flicking with the right hand while the left hand creates dynamic vibratos by pressing the strings. Compared with the geomun-go, the sound of the gayageum is clear and more stately. In the early Joseon Dynasty, both geomun-go and gayageum were played in the Rite to Royal Ancestors, but they were excluded at a later date.

Haegeum AND *Ajaeng*

The haegeum is a bowed chordophone with a smallish bamboo sound box and two strings attached to a vertical bamboo neck that is short enough to hold in one's arms. When played, varied sounds are produced by freely drawing the loose-haired bow across the loosely stretched strings. In contrast to the bowed instruments of other countries that have a soundboard made of animal skin or a large piece of wood, the small

Ajaeng

Haegeum

bamboo resonator produces the rather dry yet attractive sound characteristic of the haegeum. The ajaeng is an unusual instrument that is rested on the floor like a gayageum but played by rubbing the strings with a rosined wooden rod. This instrument exists in no Northeast Asian country other than Korea. For a long time, the ajaeng took a supportive role in providing the low notes in court music ensembles, but since the mid-20th century, the dramatic musical effect of its rough yet fresh sound has been used in a variety of contexts such as recitals and theater music. In the Rite to Royal Ancestors, the *haegeum* plays a melody similar to that of the wind instruments while the *ajaeng* supports the melody in the low register.

BAMBOO SOUND

The bamboo category includes various wind instruments. As bamboo is abundant, varied, and easy to obtain and to work with, bamboo instruments are commonly used around the world wherever bamboo grows naturally. In the "eight sounds" classification used in ancient aak, instruments made of bamboo were associated with the high, clear sounds of spring or the singing of a bird of good omen. The sound produced through the holes of the bamboo had an image of peace and harmony.

In early aak performance, five bamboo instruments—the *yak*, *jeok*, *ji*, *so*, and *gwan*—were played, and this tradition has been handed down to contemporary Korea in the Rite to Confucius. Among these, the yak and ji are transverse flutes while the jeok and gwan are vertical flutes, and the so is a set of panpipes with or without a wooden frame. Except for the so, all these instruments have a very similar tone color and musical expression regardless of the differences in their structure and playing techniques.

In addition to the aforementioned instruments, wind instruments such as the *daegeum*, *piri*, *sogeum*, *tungso*, and *danso* have unique tone colors and playing methods and occupy their own unique place in various ensembles and solo instrumental music. The daegeum and piri in particular take an important role by providing the main melody in ensembles.

Among all bamboo instruments, the yak is perhaps the leading wind instrument for aak performance. Interestingly, the Chinese character for yak describes the structure and characteristics of the instrument. The character "*yak*" is formed from the characters for "*juk*" (bamboo) and "*yak*" (pipe), with the character "*gu*" (mouth) repeated three times in a row. These "mouths" indicate the finger holes of a wind instrument. This also explains the gloss on the character "*yak*" as found in the old Chinese dictionaries, which state that "three finger holes could harmonize all sounds." This implies that the aak instrument *yak* made from bamboo was the instrument among all wind instruments that best represented the harmony of music.

It is also notable that the yak is used not only to play music but also as a prop when dancing Ilmu (the ceremonial line dance) in the Confucian sacrificial rites. Traditional Confucian rites epitomized the ancient world view held among the people of Northeast Asia. In this view, the rite expresses, through music and dance, the concept of *ye* (courtesy or ceremony) that upholds an ideal order between the universe, politics, and

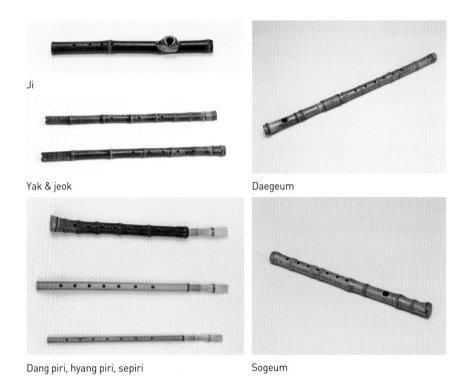

Ji

Yak & jeok

Daegeum

Dang piri, hyang piri, sepiri

Sogeum

society, as well as the concept of *ak* (music) that prevents the order from becoming too rigid by facilitating harmony among its elements. For this, a variety of musical instruments and ceremonial props are used. Among them, the yak, both used in musical performance and held in the left hand when performing the civil dance, expresses a dancing movement that symbolizes harmonious music.

The yak is made of a bamboo tube 55.3 centimeters long with a mouth hole and finger holes. The playing technique of the *yak* is little different from that of the other main wind instruments. However, because it has only three finger holes, to play aak that uses all 12 chromatic notes the player is required to use a delicate playing method in which only about a quarter of the finger hole is closed.

Among the five wind instruments that play in aak, the so has the most distinctive appearance. Unlike other wind instruments which produce several notes from a pipe by using a number of finger holes, the so is a "multi-pipe" instrument that produces only a single note from each pipe and plays a melody by using multiple pipes arranged in a row. Depending on the method of arranging the pipes, the so is divided into the *bongso* and the *baeso*. The bongso is named after a phoenix-shaped wooden frame into which the pipes are wedged, while the term "baeso" refers to the right-angled triangle shape in which the pipes are arranged alone without a frame. Both baeso and bongso are further subdivided into three types according to shape: single-winged, double-winged, and horizontal. In Korea, a double-winged bongso pipe has been in use since the 16th century. The bongso is constructed from 16 bamboo pipes held in a wooden frame. The top of each pipe is carved into a U shape to create the mouth holes, while the base is sealed with beeswax. The pitch of each pipe is adjusted by inserting a beeswax filling.

Gourd Sound

The only instrument that comes under this category is the *saeng-hwang*, a multi-pipe wind instrument with a small, round wind-chest on which bamboo pipes of differing lengths are mounted. The reason the saenghwang is classified within the gourd section is that originally a gourd was used for making the wind-chest. Although there are cases found in the world where gourds are used as percussion instruments, it is unusual to find the gourd used as a wind-chest. Moreover, from a practical viewpoint, a wind-chest made of gourd is fragile and difficult to store for long periods, while it is not yet possible to produce gourds of a regular size artificially. For these reasons, in practice the gourd wind-chest is often replaced with wood or brass. Even so, it is very remarkable that the category of "gourd" has remained in the instrument classification system for several thousand years.

In many respects, the saenghwang is an instrument that embodies a number of symbolisms associated with the traditions of Northeast Asia.

Sanghwang

The saenghwang was equated with the "sound of life" because of its appearance, in which the multiple bamboo pipes sticking out from the wind-chest suggest a scene of all the living creatures sprouting up in the spring sun; whereas the mechanism of producing sound simultaneously from a number of pipes was identified with the "sound of spring" that brings forth new life.

In the saenghwang, a free metal reed is placed in the end of each pipe within the wind-chest. The metallic timbre produced by these reeds creates a very delicate and soft sound while passing through the bamboo pipes. It also produces a harmonic effect as a result of two or more notes being sounded simultaneously. This is the most distinctive feature of the saenghwang. In general, melodic instruments of East Asia produce their sound from vegetable substances rather than metal, and their playing techniques involve sustaining a note for a long time or modifying it with vibrato rather than putting several notes together to create a harmonic effect. From that point of view, the saenghwang has been classified from ancient times as an instrument with a unique sound, and it took on a special image as its unique sound became associated with the cries of mythical animals such as the phoenix or dragon. Old poems written in Chinese often depict the sound of the saenghwang with poetic expressions such as *bonggwan* (phoenix pipes), *bongsaeng* (phoenix mouth organ), or *suryong-eum* (cry of the water dragon). Thus it can be inferred that people had special expectations toward the sound of the saenghwang, as if it were the embodiment of the phoenix.

Moreover, the mysterious associations of the saenghwang had been further intensified by its appearance in the Chinese myth of the creation of humankind by Yeowa in ancient times. Yeowa was the goddess of creation who appeared after the creation of heaven and earth and created human beings by shaping them from yellow clay. She was also the goddess of marriage who made it possible for human beings to carry on their family line by acting as a match-maker. Yeowa brought peace to humankind when it fell into chaos and disaster, and created the saenghwang and its music for her beloved humans' pleasure. Together with the shape of the instrument that depicts a phoenix's wings, the timbre that delicately blends sounds from metallic and vegetable materials, and the harmonic capability that produces two or three notes simultaneously, the appearance of the saenghwang in this ancient Northeast Asian myth, as the first musical gift to humankind from their creator, gives strong evidence of the historical and cultural symbolism associated with the saenghwang in the East Asian cultural sphere.

In addition, the saenghwang was sometimes depicted in the decorated bells or paintings of Buddhist temples as the instrument of heavenly beings, expressing the beauty of paradise, or as an instrument played by Taoist hermits with supernatural powers. The saenghwang was brought to Korea with its associated symbolism some time before the sixth century, and was maintained mainly as an instrument of court music. From around the 18th century, however, the instrument came to be appreciated in upper-class cultural circles. In the process, a style of performance called "Saengso byeongju," a duet with the clear-toned flute danso, was created. From the 20th century, however, the saenghwang was excluded from the performance of the Rite to Confucius and the Rite to Royal Ancestors.

Earth Sound

The instruments of the "earth" category are represented by the *hun* (globular ocarina made of clay) and the percussion instrument *bu* (a jar of baked clay). Like earthenware ceramics, the hun and bu are shaped from clay and then baked. Thus, they are instruments that maintain a practice from an early period of human history whereby daily utensils were created by shaping clay. These types of instrument have a long history and are still performed today as folk instruments in every corner of the world. According to the Chinese classic *Shih Ching* (*Book of Songs*), the hun and bu had been handed down as important instruments in Northeast Asia from ancient times. Since then, they have been transmitted down through the ages and used as indispensable instruments for aak.

Being made of clay, the hun and bu embodied the traditional image of the land and earth that bring forth and sustain life. Thus, the sound of musical instruments made of clay, when played well, was considered as the sound of the great wide earth itself, which would make listeners think of something noble and magnanimous. In terms of seasons, it was considered the sound of Ipchu, the onset of autumn.

The hun is a kind of enclosed small jar resembling the shape of *jeoulchu* weights. Its bottom is flat and its shape narrows toward the top. When baking the hun, a milky glaze is applied to give a luster to its color and finish. In Korea, the traditional color was black. There are six finger holes. When playing the hun, both hands hold the jar and the desired pitch is obtained by opening or closing the holes. The timbre, as one might expect

Hun   Bu

of a sound coming out of a small hole in a closed jar, is somewhat hushed and dark, with a gloomy yet gentle tone that imparts a feeling of mystery.

The hun was introduced to Korea along with aak in 1116, but today it is played only in the Rite to Confucius. In the simple, syllabic melodic progression of *Munmyo jeryeak*, the timbre of the hun contributes to the unique and mysterious image of the music. Especially, the combination of the hun and another wind instrument, the *ji* (a short transverse flute), which play together in the Rite to Confucius, embodies the meaning of "*hunji sanghwa*" (harmony of hun and ji) which appears in the classics as a symbol of brotherly love.

The bu, a percussion instrument within the "earth" category of the "eight sounds," is played in the courtyard ensemble of aak. In the past, several such vessels of different pitch were made to play melodies, but today the bu is used as a simple percussion instrument without definite pitch. Although the sound of the bu, produced by striking the rim with a split bamboo stick, is not loud, it plays an important role in contributing a unique sense of rhythm to the otherwise plain performance of aak. The bu is played only in the Rite to Confucius.

Skin Sound

This category includes numerous kinds of drums. In all continents and cultures of the world, drums are manufactured and performed in a variety of different ways. In Korea, there are about 40 different kinds of traditional percussion instruments that are used in court music, Confucian rites, Buddhist music, military music, and folk music. In ancient society, the drum was often used as a signaling device. Its importance for giving signals in warfare is indicated by a Korean proverb: "A commander who knows how to handle soldiers will sound the drum before the sound of gunfire." A drum housed in the city center was used to strike each hour, while people who had been mistreated could plead for mercy by beating a drum called the "*sinmun-go*" (petitioner's drum). On the other hand, the "*joeinui buk*" (sinner's drum) was strapped to the back of criminals, who would be forced to carry it through the streets beating it loudly, thus achieving the effect of "*ilbeolbaekgye*" (warning a hundred people by punishing one).

From ancient times, the drum has also been a symbol of sacrifice. Many anecdotes appear in the ancient myths of Northeast Asia which state that in order to demonstrate their authority, the creators of humankind played a drum made from the skin of the biggest animal on earth. In addition, the belief that the sound of drumming could mediate between heaven and earth led to the tradition of beating a drum made of animal skin whenever presenting a sacrificial rite to the gods. Thus, the drum was both an object of sacrifice in praying for a peaceful life for humankind, and at the same time, a symbolic object that had the significance of an altar for offering those prayers.

Drums for sacrificial rites, manufactured on the basis of ancient East Asian thought and handed down to the present time, are abundantly imbued with symbolism and meaning. A wooden stand for a drum decorated with crouching tigers facing in four directions in a cross shape, or with carvings of a dragon, phoenix, heron, or moon, symbolizes the belief that the imposing image and sound of a drum communicates with the universe and nature. Special colors or designs are applied to the frame at the point where the drums are attached, or to the wooden body of the drum itself, to express the idea that the sound of the drum is in harmony with nature.

Among all the drums, the largest and most splendid is the barrel drum *geon-go*. The geon-go is a "standing drum" with a cross-shaped base in

Jeolgo & jin-go

Jwago

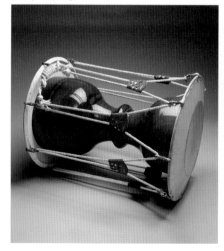
Janggu

Nodo & nogo

the form of four crouching tigers facing in the four directions. A wooden pole strong enough to support a large drum stands on this base and the drum is fixed to it. To add to the splendor, the body of the drum is painted red, or (especially for geon-go played at banquets) decorated with peony blossoms that symbolize riches, honor, and prosperity. In addition, a two-story pavilion rests on top of the drum. The lower part of pavilion is decorated with red and green silk curtains, while its four sides are painted with cloud, flower, and lotus patterns. From the top of each corner of the lower pavilion protrudes a *yonggan* or "dragon rod" carved with a dragon's head on the end, and from these hang long *yuso* (colored silk tassels) made from strings of five colors threaded through beads also of five colors. Each yuso is hung from a small iron ring in the dragon's mouth, as though the dragon were biting the yuso. The top of the drum is crowned with a soaring crane.

Compared to the *janggu* (hourglass drum), the *buk* (barrel drum) has a dull sound, but it has an air of dignity unlike the "chattering sound" produced by the thin bamboo stick of the janggu. For this reason, the buk was indispensable for ceremonial music that required a large volume or majestic effect, whether it be for sacrificial rites, court music, Buddhist temples or shamanistic rituals or folk music festivals. As reflected in expressions such as "a drumming sound to shake heaven and earth" or "a big drum makes a big sound," it has been considered imperative that a drum should produce a loud and powerful sound. Seasonally, the drumming sound was associated with mid-winter and symbolized the winter solstice that traditionally marked the beginning of a new year.

WOOD SOUND

The "wood" category includes the percussion instruments *chuk*, *bak*, and *eo*. Because it has no after-tone, the sound of struck wood gives an impression of straightness, and has traditionally been regarded as the musical expression of a righteous image. Thus, it was believed that when listening to the upright sound of wood, listeners would be led to think about what was right, and this "right thinking" would make them less greedy, thus promoting a clean state of mind. Reflecting this belief, wooden instruments were seasonally associated with the sound of Ipha, the onset of summer.

In Korean music, the short and dull sound of wooden percussion instruments was primarily used as a kind of signal rather than something for playing a rhythm. A representative example, the chuk, is a percussion instrument that looks like a mortar with a square body. Normally, green paint is applied to this wooden box, which is then decorated with a very simple landscape. When playing the chuk, a wooden pestle-like stick is struck vertically against the base of the box with three thuds: "kung kung kung." The eo has a very unique appearance representing a crouching white tiger with 27 wooden saw teeth along its spine. When playing, a stick, made of a bamboo tube split at one end, strikes the tiger's head ("ttuk ttuk ttuk") and scrapes along its back ("hududududuk"), resulting in a very distinctive percussive sound. The bak is a percussion instrument made of six thin rectangular slabs bound together like a folding fan. When playing, the wooden slabs are unfolded like the ribs of a fan and then sharply folded up together with a cracking sound like "ttak."

The chuk, eo, and bak are only played to signal the beginning and ending, or to announce an important change during the performance. The chuk and eo, in particular, have a special function in Confucian ritual music in signaling the beginning and ending of a piece. The surface of the chuk is painted green, symbolizing the east. East is the direction in which the sun rises, and incorporates the meaning of starting something new. Thus, the chuk is always placed on the eastern side of the orchestra, and when the music starts, it beats nine times: "kung-kungkung, kung-kungkung, kung-kungkung." The tiger-shaped eo, on the other hand, symbolizes the

Chuk

Eo

Bak

west and signifies the conclusion of something, and thus it is used only at the end of a piece. It is played by striking the tiger's head three times and scraping its spine three times, the whole pattern being repeated three times.

Thus, the principal "wood sound" instruments chuk and eo play a limited role in musical performance as signals of the beginning and ending. Nevertheless, they display time-honored East Asian philosophical concepts through musical performance by signifying, respectively, east and west, beginning and ending, yang and yin, as well as expressing the symbolism of the perfect number, nine, in the number of strokes played. As for the bak, it is played in court music ensembles and dance accompaniment as well as aak to signal the beginning and ending of a piece as well as changes of tempo or dance movement. Normally, the bak is played once at the beginning of an ensemble piece and three times at the end. The crisp sound of the bak striking "tak tak tak" without after-tones starts and finishes the majestic ensemble pieces in grand style. The bak player in the sacrificial rites and court dances has a special title, *jipbak*, and is generally the leader of the ensemble who performs the role of conductor.

APPENDIX III

**The score of the "Yeongsin Huimun" Section of
the "Botaepyeong-jiak," the Song for Welcoming the Gods**

The score of "Somu," the First Piece of the "Jeongdaeeop-jiak" Song